The Portable

Jewish Mother

GUILT, FOOD, AND...WHEN ARE YOU
GIVING ME GRANDCHILDREN?

Laurie Rozakis, Ph.D.

Adams Media
Avon, Massachusetts

Published by
Adams Media, an F+W Publications Company
57 Littlefield Street, Avon, MA 02322. U.S.A.
www.adamsmedia.com

Printed in the United States of America.
J I H G F E D C B A

Library of Congress Cataloging-in-Publication Data

Rozakis, Laurie.
The portable Jewish mother / Laurie Rozakis.
p. cm.
ISBN-13: 978-1-59869-341-6
ISBN-10: 1-59869-341-7
1. Mothers—Humor. 2. Jewish women—Humor. I. Title.
PN6231.M68R69 2007
818'.602—dc22   2006102184

This publication is designed to provide accurate and authoritative information
with regard to the subject matter covered. It is sold with the understanding that
the publisher is not engaged in rendering legal, accounting, or other professional
advice. If legal advice or other expert assistance is required, the services of a
competent professional person should be sought.

—From a *Declaration of Principles* jointly adopted by a Committee of the
American Bar Association and a Committee of Publishers and Associations

Many of the designations used by manufacturers and sellers to distinguish their
product are claimed as trademarks. Where those designations appear in this
book and Adams Media was aware of a trademark claim, the designations have
been printed with initial capital letters.

Interior illustration: Kathie Kelleher
Interior photography: challahh bread: ©iStockphoto.com/Dawn Lilgenquist;
can opener: ©iStockphoto.com/Mike Wigins; open can: ©iStockphoto.com/
Sean Locke; measuring spoons: ©iStockphoto.com/Rich Koele; bagels: ©iStock
photo.com/lushmedia; wooden spoon ©iStockphoto.com/jcphoto; measuring
cup©iStockphoto.com/ancci

This book is available at quantity discounts for bulk purchases.
For information, please call 1-800-289-0963.

Dedication

To WTG, whose wonderful feisty Jewish mother Leah had the pleasure of knowing her son is a real mensch.

—As ever and always,
Laurie

Acknowledgments

My deepest thanks to the generous and gracious friends who shared their thoughts, memories, and analyses with me. Each and every one of you helped me crystallize my ideas and present a balanced and fair view of an epic subject.

My angels include:

Emily Bengels
Professor Barbara Bengels
Dorrie Berkowitz
Jeri Cipriano
Jessica Conklin
Jillian Dorans
Michael Ebert
Dr. Leslie Friedman
Margie Glazer
Alan Gold
Betty Gold
Chaya Goldish
Meish Goldish
Gary Goldstein
Mark Goros
Nita Goros
Bob Greenberger
Mona Lanzer
Peter Lanzer
Amy Losi
Judy Klau Pace
Judith Pasko
Martin Pasko
Barbara Rogan
Charles Rozakis
Samantha Rozakis
Erica Saviuk
Jodi Saviuk
Dr. Ann Shapiro
Judy Smith
Pessha Snedecker
Mary Ellen Snodgrass
Dr. Michael Steinman
Michelle Stern

Contents

Introduction

For those of you who don't have the benefit of a real Jewish mother, not to worry: You have *The Portable Jewish Mother*. Now you can carry advice and guilt with you all the time. (. . . *you're not actually going outside wearing that, are you?*)

Of course, you don't have to be either Jewish or a mother to be a Jewish mother. This book is for all mothers, Jewish or not. (*Would it kill you to pick up the phone and call your mother?*)

As my friend Meish Goldish says: A Jewish mother is a bundle of contradictions.

On the one hand, she is impossible to please. She'll give you two ties as gifts, and when you put one of them on, she'll ask, "What's wrong? You don't like the other one?"

On the other hand, a Jewish mother is also an eternal optimist. She tells her friends, "My son is gay, but thank God he's dating a nice Jewish doctor."

A Jewish mother is always proud, even in her naiveté. "My son is so successful," she boasts, "and I'm so happy. He goes to a therapist. He pays $300 a session. And all he talks about is me, me, me!"

Yet a Jewish mother is also savvy. She tells her daughter, "What do you mean you're pregnant? And you don't even know the father's name? Didn't it ever occur to you to turn to the man and say, 'Excuse me, but with whom am I having the pleasure?'"

In short, a Jewish mother is an eternal pain and an eternal blessing. Jewish mother Judy Smith says: "A Jewish mother means loving and feeding your children in excess, keeping them close to home from the time they are born, running their lives till they leave home, hearing from them more than once a day, loving and being loved by their wives."

As I say: Jewish mothers, we take credit for what we do wrong, but we rarely take credit for what we do right. And we do a lot right. So give yourself some credit already.

Meet the Mishpocha

(Family)

For a Jewish mother, family is all.
So let's meet the family.

Test Your J.Q. (Jewish Quotient)

Let's start with the basics: How much do you know about Jewish mothers and the chosen people? Take this simple test to see.

Part 1: True/False

Directions: Circle *true* or *false* for each statement.

1. Katie Couric, the newscaster, has a Jewish mother. This makes her Jewish. As the mother of two daughters, she's a Jewish mother.

   True   False

2. *Goy* is the Yiddish term for a person who is not Jewish. Jewish mothers use it like this: "She's a goy, but she *can* cook."

   True   False

3. A Jewish mother's e-mail reads: "Begin worrying. Details to follow."

   True   False

4. A ham sandwich with mayo is not kosher, even if it *is* served on matzoh with a sour dill pickle. A Jewish mother wouldn't serve it.

   True   False

5. Kate Hudson and Gwyneth Paltrow are real, genuine Jewish mothers.

   True   False

Eat Your Pickles

The Torah doesn't have much to say about pickles: Pickles are, after all, vegetables, which the dietary laws don't cover. Nonetheless, Jewish mothers want you to eat pickles because they are vegetables.

Part 2: Multiple Choice

Directions: Circle the letter of the correct choice.

6 According to a Jewish mother, when does a Jewish fetus become viable?

    A. at conception

    B. at three months

    C. at six months

    D. when he graduates from medical school

7 Which of the following actresses is NOT a Jewish mother?

    A. Lauren Bacall

    B. Joan Rivers

    C. Debra Winger

    D. Madonna

8 What did the waiter ask the group of Jewish mothers as they ate their dinners?

    A. "So, what's new by you?"

B. "Do you eat anything but lettuce?"

C. "Would you like some fries with that?"

D. "Is ANYTHING all right?"

9 According to a Jewish mother, which is the definition of *chutzpah*?

    A. A suspiciously evasive answer to an inquiry, usually with the implication that the question is either being purposely avoided or is downright silly.

    B. A traditional dish involving fish, carrots, parsley, and something else better left unidentified.

    C. What happens when you try to eat a stale bagel with new dentures.

    D. A man who kills his mother and father and then throws himself on the mercy of the court because he's an orphan.

10 Moshe is talking to his psychiatrist. "I had a weird dream last night," he says. "I saw my mother but then I noticed she had your face. I found this so upsetting that I immediately awoke and couldn't get back to sleep. I sat up thinking about the dream until 7 A.M. Then I got up, made myself a slice of toast and some coffee, and came straight here. Can you please help me explain the meaning of my dream?"

What did the psychiatrist say?

    A. "You should try maybe a glass of hot milk."

    B. "Your time is up. Same time, next week?"

    C. "You are one weird dude."

    D. "One slice of toast and coffee? Do you call that a breakfast?"

⓫ Which of the following *Star Trek* actors is NOT Jewish (hence, not the son of a Jewish mother)?

    A. William Shatner (Captain James T. Kirk)

    B. Leonard Nimoy (Spock)

    C. Brent Spiner (Data)

    D. George Takei (Lieutenant Sulu)

⓬ When a Jewish mother prepares a meal for a family of five, the actual number of people she prepares food for is:

    A. 5

    B. 6

    C. 8

    D. the population of New York City

⓭ When he grows up, your Jewish son is LEAST likely to be

    A. a rabbi

    B. a lawyer

    C. an accountant

    D. a football player

14 Why don't Jewish mothers drink?

    A. Booze is fattening.

    B. Who has time?

    C. Have *you* ever tasted Manischewitz wine?

    D. Alcohol interferes with their suffering.

15 Why do Jewish mothers make such great parole officers?

    A. They always show mercy.

    B. They obey the law.

    C. They would keep the jail floor clean enough to eat off it.

    D. They never let anyone finish a sentence.

Manischewitz

The B. Manischewitz Company, founded in 1888 in Cincinnati, Ohio, is a leading manufacturer of kosher products in the United States: The company sells the most matzoh and the most kosher wine in America. Manischewitz products are always featured on a Jewish mother's table during the holidays.

16 Which food is a Jewish mother LEAST likely to order as take-out from a Jewish deli?

    A. a pastrami on rye

    B. a slab of strawberry cheesecake

C. potato pancakes with apple sauce

D. a five-pound Maine lobster with drawn butter

⑰ Which of these couples is LEAST likely to attend Friday night services at shul?

    A. Mr. and Mrs. Samuel Feinstein

    B. Mr. and Mrs. Leopold Bloom

    C. Mr. and Mrs. Steven Machtinger

    D. Mr. and Mrs. Mel Gibson

⑱ Which of the following is not a traditional bagel variety?

    A. poppy

    B. onion

    C. sesame

    D. Hellman's

⑲ If you're Jewish, the person you're MOST likely to tell your therapist about is

    A. your lover

    B. your roommate

    C. your cat

    D. your mother

⑳ If you're Jewish, you should call your mother

    A. annually

    B. monthly

    C. weekly

    D. every single day, and twice on weekends

Part 3: Essay

Directions: How can you tell the difference between an Italian mother, a French mother, and a Jewish mother? Write your answer on a separate piece of paper.

Answers

#1–#5 Every answer is *true*.

#6–#20 Every answer is D.

Sample Essay

Three women—an Italian woman, a French woman, and a Jewish mother—are condemned to be executed. Their captors tell them that they have the right to have a final meal before the execution. They ask the French woman what she wants.

"Give me the best French wine, French bread, and French cheese," she requests as she powders her nose.

So they give it to her, she eats it, and then they execute her. Next it's the Italian's turn.

"Give me a great big plate of pasta with red sauce and meatballs," says the Italian woman. So they bring it to her, she eats it, and then they execute her. Now it's the Jewish mother's turn.

"I want a big bowl of strawberries," says the Jewish mother.

"Strawberries? They aren't even in season!" her captors reply.

"So I'll wait . . ." the Jewish mother replies.

Score Yourself
15–20 correct: I'll bet that everyone cheated off your homework in Hebrew school, even smarty-pants Danny Kaplan.

14–10 correct: So you cut Hebrew School to play Game Boy, eh? You knew you'd pay some day, but who knew that day would come so soon?

9–5 correct: You never saw a Woody Allen movie?

Fewer than 5 correct: Your elementary school teacher was Sister Anna Maria Theresa Christina at Our Lady of the Perpetual Nosebleed.

Overview of Judaism
Before we can explore the notion of Jewish mothers, we've got to settle on what makes someone Jewish. This is not as easy as you might think.

In general, Jews are people who follow the beliefs of Judaism, but more on that later. At this time, there are about 14.5 million Jews. Most Jews live in America and in Israel, the Jewish state. Currently, the largest Jewish community in the world is located in the United States, with almost 5.7 million Jews. There are also large Jewish populations in Canada and Argentina, and smaller populations in Brazil, Mexico, Uruguay, Venezuela, Chile, and several other countries.

The origin of the Jewish people is traditionally dated to around 1800 B.C.E. with the biblical account of the birth of Judaism. The English word "Jew" comes from the biblical word *Yehudi*, first used in the Book of Esther to refer to the Jewish people. Notice that the book refers to a Jewish mother.

Who's a Jew?

Jews are a nation, an ethnicity, a religion, and a culture—much more than merely following a set of religious guidelines. The following guidelines will help you get a handle on how "being Jewish" is defined.

1. Jews are people who practice Judaism.
2. Jews are people who consider themselves Jews even if they don't practice Judaism. They identify themselves as Jewish by virtue of their family's Jewish descent and their own cultural and historical beliefs. Thus, people can be deeply Jewish without being religious. This is not uncommon at all.
3. Jews are people who have a Jewish background.
4. Jews are people who have converted to Judaism.

Israel

The State of Israel was proclaimed on May 14, 1948. A parliamentary democracy, Israel is the world's only Jewish state—although its population includes citizens from many different ethnic and religious backgrounds. Jewish mothers often work to support Israel through service organizations such as Hadassah.

According to *halacha* (Jewish law and traditions), only a child born to a Jewish mother is counted as Jewish. A child with a

Jewish father and a non-Jewish mother is considered a non-Jew. More on this later.

Jewish denominations that don't accept Orthodox views of Jewish law have different standards for determining Jewishness, of course. American Reform Judaism and British Liberal Judaism, for instance, accept the child of one Jewish parent (father or mother) as Jewish if the parents raise the child as a Jew by Progressive standards. If you're not lucky enough to have a Jewish parent or two and decide that conversion is the way to go, not to worry: All mainstream forms of Judaism today accept converts. And those converts are treated just the same as those born into the tribe. The convert is as much a Jew as anyone born Jewish.

Therefore, mere *belief* in the principles of Judaism does *not* make you Jewish. Take the following quiz to see who is considered a Jew by the rules of the religion.

● ●

Conversion to Judaism

According to the standards of Orthodox and Conservative Judaism, children who have converted are asked when they reach their legal majority (twelve years old for a girl, thirteen years old for a boy) if they wish to remain Jewish.

● ●

12

The Portable Jewish Mother

Choose the Chosen People

Directions: Circle *yes* or *no* for each statement.

1. A woman we'll call "Sunshine Raindrop Peace" was born to hippy non-Jewish parents in a San Francisco vegan commune. Sunshine Raindrop Peace has not undergone the formal process of conversion to Judaism, but she nonetheless observes every law of Orthodox Judaism and believes all the doctrine. She never misses a Friday night service at synagogue and celebrates all Jewish holidays according to the rules. She's even the second assistant vice president of Hadassah at her temple and chairwoman of the annual Casino Night to benefit Israel. She has three sons who all play varsity football and drive motorcycles. Is Sunshine Raindrop Peace a Jewish mother?

    Yes   No

2. A woman we'll call "Frances" was born to a Jewish mother who is an atheist. Mama never practices Judaism at all and certainly didn't bring Frances up as Jewish. No bas mitzvah (coming-of-age ceremony). The family celebrates Christmas all the way: They put up a real Christmas tree, welcome the jolly fat man bearing gifts, display tacky lawn ornaments, and serve a loin of pork marinated in gin. Frances is married to an Episcopalian man named Wade, who starches his underwear and wears a suit and tie every night

to dinner. They have two handsome and talented sons who have done exceedingly well in school, thank you very much. Is Frances a Jewish mother?

Yes   No

3. A woman we'll call "Deborah Beth" was born Jewish, but never practiced the religion and married a Catholic man named Vito de Jesus. She converted to Catholicism for her wedding. She and Vito have fifteen children, nine neutered cats, six asthmatic fish, two terrified gerbils, and a large slobbery dog who regularly tries to eat the gerbils. Is Deborah Beth a Jewish mother?

Yes   No

4. A woman we'll call "Madonna" was born Roman Catholic, educated by nuns, and became a nun herself. Soon after, however, Madonna had a change of heart and underwent a formal conversion to Judaism. She changed her last name to Finkelstein, married a man named David Shapiro-Roth, and had four children. Is Madonna Finkelstein-Shapiro-Roth a Jewish mother?

Yes   No

Answers

1. Sorry, Sunshine Raindrop Peace, you're still a goy (non-Jew). Religion aside, that detail about "three sons who all play varsity football and drive motorcycles" is a valuable

14

The Portable Jewish Mother

tip-off. Real Jewish mothers would never let their sons or daughters play contact sports. And ride motorcycles? Better you should rip out a Jewish mother's heart and stomp on it right now.

2. Frances is a Jew. Mama is a Jewish mother, so Frances is a Jewish mother.

3. Once a Jew, always a Jew. Deborah Beth is still a Jew, according to the laws of Judaism. And with fifteen kids and a passel of pets, we'd award Deborah the crown of Jewish motherhood anyway to salute her stamina. But this couple needs another hobby. Maybe they should get a big-screen television.

4. Madonna Finkelstein-Shapiro-Roth is now a Jewish mother. Conversions take. But that hyphenated name will be an issue when the kids fill out the forms for their SATs.

Thus, as this quiz demonstrates, the immediate descendants of all female Jews are still considered to be Jews, as are all her female descendants. Second, even those descendants who are not aware they are Jews, or practice a faith other than Judaism, are technically still Jews, as long as they come from an unbroken female line of descent. This makes for more Jewish mothers.

The Clan of Buba

Perhaps the most unlikely Jews are the Lemba, 70,000 black people from southern Africa. They speak Bantu as the other local tribes do, but the Lemba follow Jewish customs and beliefs that have been transmitted orally for hundreds of years. Don't believe they're Jews? We've got genetic proof. More than half the men in the tribe's Buba clan carry a genetic marker found among Jewish priests, the Kohanim. (The word *Kohanim* is today's surname *Cohen*.) So there are black African Jewish mothers.

Jews are generally divided into two main categories, depending on their backgrounds. The categories are *Ashkenazi Jews* and *Sephardi Jews*. The terms refer to both religious and ethnic divisions. There are other divisions as well, but these are the major divisions in America.

Ashkenazi Jews

Ashkenazi Jews are those who trace their roots to Central Europe. Use this memory trick to make it easy to figure out who's who: *Ashkenazi* means "German" in Hebrew. Although in the eleventh century they comprised only 3 percent of the world's Jewish population, today Ashkenazi Jews account for approximately 80 percent of the world's Jews. Not surprisingly, most Jews in America are Ashkenazi Jews, because they can trace their roots to Europe. Thus, most Jewish mothers are Ashkenazi.

Below is a list of famous Ashkenazi Jews, including some of the most famous Ashkenazi Jewish mothers. On the lines provided, explain why each one is famous.

1. Menachem Begin _____
2. Leonard Bernstein _____
3. Niels Bohr _____
4. George Burns _____
5. Tony Curtis, Jamie Lee Curtis _____
6. Bob Dylan _____
7. Albert Einstein _____
8. Franz Kafka _____
9. Henry Kissinger _____
10. Groucho Marx _____
11. Felix Mendelssohn _____
12. Golda Meir _____
13. Zero Mostel _____
14. Natalie Portman _____
15. Gilda Radner _____
16. Edward G. Robinson _____
17. Aaron Spelling _____
18. Mark Spitz _____

Answers

1. Menachem Begin: former prime minister of Israel
2. Leonard Bernstein: composer
3. Niels Bohr: nuclear physicist
4. George Burns: classic comedian
5. Tony Curtis, Jamie Lee Curtis: actors (father and daughter). In addition to being an actor and a Jewish mother, Jamie Lee Curtis is the author of several children's books.
6. Bob Dylan: hangdog musician
7. Albert Einstein: greatest scientist of the twentieth century; mathematician, physicist, humanitarian
8. Franz Kafka: paranoid writer
9. Henry Kissinger: statesman
10. Groucho Marx: actor

Bet You Didn't Know

Tony Curtis, born Bernard Schwarz, is the father of famous Jewish mother Jamie Lee Curtis. The handsome icon of twentieth-century Hollywood cinema was the star of several classic movies, including *The Sweet Smell of Success* (1957) and *Some Like It Hot* (1959, with Jack Lemmon and Marilyn Monroe). Curtis is also an accomplished painter who has art shows all over the world.

11. Felix Mendelssohn: composer
12. Golda Meir: former prime minister of Israel. She's such an important Jewish mother that you'll read her entire biography later in this book.
13. Zero Mostel: actor
14. Natalie Portman: actress, but too young yet to be a Jewish mother
15. Gilda Radner: actor, but tragically died before she had a chance to become a Jewish mother
16. Edward G. Robinson: actor
17. Aaron Spelling: producer; father of Jewish mother Tori Spelling
18. Mark Spitz: Olympic swimming champion

Sephardic Jews

Sephardic Jews hail from Spain, Portugal, and North Africa. Here's your memory jog: *Sephardic* means "Spanish" in Hebrew. Both words start with *s*. The Sephardic Jews are descendants of Jews who left Spain or Portugal after the 1492 expulsion of the Jews. The Sephardic Jews preserved their special language, a combination of Hebrew and Spanish known as *Ladino*. Ladino is still spoken by some Sephardic communities, such as those in Greece, Turkey, Bulgaria, Rumania, France, and Latin America.

Sephardic and Ashkenazi Jews share the same tenets of Judaism and use the same Bible. Differences arise in customs and in liturgy. For example, on Passover, Ashkenazi Jews eat matzoh and products made from matzoh meal, while Sephardic Jews eat rice and corn products.

The Marx Brothers

The Marx Brothers—real brothers—were a team of comedians who began their career in vaudeville and stage plays and then went on to movies and TV. They each had a stage name. The best known were Groucho (Julius, 1890–1977), Harpo (Adolph, 1888–1964), and Chico (Leonard, 1887–1961). The act also included Gummo (Milton, 1892–1997) and Zeppo (Herbert, 1901–1979). If you haven't seen their movies, stop reading immediately and rent *Duck Soup, Horse Feathers, A Night at the Opera*, and *A Day at the Races*. And thank their Jewish mother for nurturing such talented boys.

In the next chapter, you'll read about some famous Jewish mothers. I've included some Jewish men, too, just so they don't kvetch (complain) that they never get any attention.

CHAPTER 2

Famous Jewish Mothers

(and Some Famous Jewish Men, So They Don't Write Me Kvetchy Letters)

What do Bette Midler, Goldie Hawn, and Judy Blume all have in common? Only the first two are actresses. Here's the commonality: they're all Jewish mothers. You'll be astonished to learn how many notable women are genuine Jewish mothers.

My friend Jeri Cipriano defined a Jewish mother based on first-hand observation—her own beloved mother:

My father died when I was seven and my mother remained a widow until ninety-one. We were close. Thank you for the opportunity to think of all her mishegoss. [Literally, "insanity, madness," but often used playfully to mean "amusing trouble."] Jewish mothers love unconditionally and mine used to remind me that she was both mother and father to me (so you can imagine the guilt).

Mishegoss

As you just read, *mishegoss* means "insanity," but its general use is indulgent rather than specific or critical. Here's an example: "Such mishegoss my Jewish mother gives me. She wants me to marry Irving the cantor. Ah, but I love Morris the plumber."

Famous Jewish Mothers in Entertainment

Adam Sandler has hit it big with his Hanukkah songs, and rightly so: They're a hoot. The songs list famous Jews. As Sandler noted in his song, female Jewish actresses are a fine-looking crew in general. Even more important, they're strong, successful role models who bring pride to the tribe. How much do you know about the following Jewish mothers in show biz?

* **Debra Messing of *Will & Grace* fame** drew on her own Jewish mother-ness to create the character of Grace Adler. Messing said in an interview, "There are a lot of Jews around on the set and we have fun. I'm Jewish and, I think, it's just a sensibility that they write. They write it, and I recognize it because it's a part of my family, my history and my language, so there is a rhythm to it that's familiar to me and it's fun to play."

* **Alicia Silverstone** of *Clueless* fame grew up a good Jewish girl and is very proud of her Jewish heritage. "My family attended Temple Beth Jacob. I was reared in a traditional Jewish household," Silverstone recalls. "We lit candles Friday night and had seders. My brother David and I went to Hebrew school and had our bar mitzvahs. I have wonderful memories of my bat mitzvah." Silverstone's father is a Jew who hails from London. He resettled in God's waiting room—Florida—where he met his wife Didi. A Christian, she worked for Pan Am as a flight attendant. Before the marriage, Didi converted, so Alicia was born a Jew. Alicia received much of her formal Jewish education by attending shul (synagogue) with her elderly grandfather Sidney Silver.

* **Joan Collins** is also a nice Jewish girl. At birth, she was named Joan Henrietta Collins. She hails from Bayswater.

And my favorite all-time Jewish mother in show biz: **Betty Joan Perske**. You know her as Lauren Bacall. She's a Jewish mother three times over!

Lauren Bacall

Lauren Bacall (born in 1924) is famous for her husky voice and sultry looks. A role model for modern-day women, Jewish or not, she is a legendary actress. Bacall is best known for being a film noir leading lady in *The Big Sleep* (1946) and *Dark Passage* (1947), as well as a sassy comedienne, as seen in *How to Marry a Millionaire* (1953). I also admire her for her courageous outspokenness, a quality most Jewish mothers possess, as you'll read about later. Here are some of her most famous pronouncements:

* **From *To Have and Have Not* (1945):** "You know you don't have to act with me, Steve. You don't have to say anything and you don't have to do anything. Not a thing. Oh, maybe just whistle. You know how to whistle, don't you, Steve? You just put your lips together and blow."
* **From *The Big Sleep*:** Humphrey Bogart: "What's wrong with you?" Lauren Bacall: "Nothing you can't fix."
* **And Bacall's comments about Tom Cruise in the August 8, 2005, issue of *Time* magazine:** "When you talk about a

great actor, you're not talking about Tom Cruise. His whole behavior is so shocking. It's inappropriate and vulgar and absolutely unacceptable to use your private life to sell anything commercially, but, I think it's kind of a sickness."

Bacall was born in New York City, the only child of Jewish immigrants William Perske (related to former Israeli Prime Minister Shimon Peres) and Natalie Weinstein-Bacal. William was a salesman; Natalie, a secretary. They divorced when Bacall was only six years old.

Bacall studied dancing and took acting lessons, working as a theater usher and model. She made her acting debut on Broadway in 1942, in a play called *Johnny Two by Four*. When she experienced anti-Semitism during the play's run, Bacall decided to conceal the fact that she was Jewish.

Bacall's big break came when Howard Hawks's wife spotted Bacall on the cover of *Harper's Bazaar* and showed the photo to her husband, who called Bacall in for a screen test. The result was *To Have and Have Not*, which catapulted Bacall to instant stardom.

She met Humphrey Bogart on the set, sparks flew, and their relationship began.

Among her films of the 1950s are *Young Man with a Horn*, costarring Doris Day and Kirk Douglas (yes, both Jewish). Then came *How to Marry a Millionaire*, also starring Marilyn Monroe (also Jewish). In the 1960s, Bacall returned to Broadway.

In 1945, Bacall married Bogie. She was twenty; he was forty-five. After Bogie's death, Bacall married Jason Robards. The marriage lasted from 1961 to 1969. Bacall gets Jewish mother status from her two sons and a daughter:

* News producer, documentary filmmaker, and author Stephen Bogart
* Actor Sam Robards
* Daughter Leslie Bogart

Jewish Mothers Who Also Acted for a Living

The following chart shows some famous female Jewish actresses from the past. How many did you know were Jewish mothers? (Bet I'll surprise you!)

The Portable Jewish Mother

Jewish Mothers in Show Biz Around the Turn of the Twentieth Century

Jewish Mother	Most Famous Roles
Stella Adler	American actress, for decades regarded as America's foremost acting teacher
Theda Bara	silent film star
Sarah Bernhardt	world-famous stage actress
Fanny Brice	comedian, the original "Funny Girl"
Molly Picone	Yiddish theater and film star
Norma Shearer	actress
Mae West	sexpot; invited men to "come up and see me sometime"

Jewish Mothers in Show Biz: 1930s–1960s

Jewish Mother	Most Famous Roles
Lauren Bacall	actress, Jewish mother of actor Sam Robards
Estelle Getty	actress who played Sophia Petrillo on *The Golden Girls*
Judy Holliday	Academy Award–winning actress known for her skill at comedy
Ali McGraw	actress most famous for her line in *Love Story*: "Love means never having to say you're sorry."

Anne Meara	a fine actress in her own right, but also the proud Jewish mother of actor Ben Stiller
Ruby Myers	Jewish-Indian film actress
Estelle Parsons	TV actress, also had a role in *Boys on the Side*
Charlotte Rae	actress who played Mrs. Garrett on *The Facts of Life*
Doris Roberts	actress who played Raymond's mother on *Everybody Loves Raymond*
Dinah Shore	actress; hostess of her own television variety show
Florence Stanley	actress (remember her as Fish's wife on *Barney Miller*?)
Shelley Winters	actress (who can forget her in the original *Poseidon Adventure*?)

Contemporary Jewish Mothers in Show Biz

Jewish Mother	Most Famous Roles
Patricia Arquette	actress (lately on TV's *Medium*)
Ellen Barkin	actress who starred in *Fear and Loathing in Las Vegas*
Barbie Benton	actress
Lisa Edelstein	actress (lately on TV's medical show *House*)

28

Jami Gertz	actress
Jennifer Grey	actress (remember her as "Baby" getting it on with Patrick Swayze in *Dirty Dancing*?)
Helen Hunt	actress
Lisa Kudrow	actress (Phoebe on *Friends*)
Julianna Margulies	actress (lucky lady: she got to cuddle with George Clooney on *ER*)
Ally Sheedy	member of the "Brat Pack"

Jennifer Grey

Jennifer Grey, the daughter of legendary actor Joel Grey, had her big break when she played Ferris's sister Jeanie in *Ferris Bueller's Day Off*. Jewish mother Jennifer Grey has one daughter, Stella, born in 2001. She is married to actor Clark Gregg.

Jews in Sports, Including Some Jewish Mothers

According to the stereotype, Jews make great doctors but lousy football players. Take the following quiz to explore this stereotype. Put a check mark next to the name of each athlete you think was fortunate enough to be a Jewish mother or have a Jewish mother.

1. Sportscaster Marv Albert
2. Major league baseball player Sandy Koufax
3. Hungarian fencer and Olympic champion Sandor Erdos
4. U.S. basketball player/coach/manager Red Auerbach
5. U.S. world champion boxer Barney Ross
6. Championship chess player Judit Polgar
7. U.S. football player Lyle Alzado
8. U.S. world champion boxer Max Baer
9. Ukrainian figure skater Oksana Baiul
10. Olympic medalist figure skater Sasha Cohen
11. Mark Cuban, owner of the Dallas Mavericks
12. U.S. football Hall of Famer Ron Mix
13. Olympic medalist figure skater Sarah Hughes
14. LPGA professional golfer Amy Alcott
15. Hockey players Bob Nystrom and his son Eric
16. Major league baseball player Craig Breslow
17. Olympic champion swimmer Anthony Erwin
18. Adam Goldberg of the Minnesota Vikings and
    St. Louis Rams
19. U.S. cross-country runner Daniel Suher
20. U.S. professional wrestler and NFL player Bill Goldberg

Answers

No fooling you: They're all members of the tribe. Yep: Every single one of them is Jewish. Some are even Jewish mothers!

Jews and Jewish Mothers in the News

Each of the people listed below is Jewish; many are Jewish mothers. This time, see if you can fill in each person's claim to fame.

Jews Most Likely to Appear in *People* Magazine

Name	Claim to Fame
J. D. Salinger	
Noah Wyle	
Jonas Salk	
Yasmine Bleeth	
Harry Houdini	
Harlan Ellison	
Dustin Hoffman	
Modigliani	
Roseanne Barr	
Judith Resnik	
Frida Kahlo	
Ayn Rand	
Neve Campbell	
Frank Gehry	
Bugsy Siegel	
Harrison Ford	

Judy Blume	
Marc Chagall	
Dutch Schultz	
Jerry Seinfeld	

Answers

Here's the key:

Jews Most Likely to Appear in *People* Magazine

Name	Claim to Fame
J. D. Salinger	author of a paean to teenage angst, *The Catcher in the Rye.* Surprisingly—given the theme of guilt—there is no Jewish mother in the novel.
Noah Wyle	an Jewish actor who plays a doctor; betcha his Jewish mother is proud!
Jonas Salk	scientist who developed the first polio vaccine
Yasmine Bleeth	actress best known so far as a *Baywatch* babe
Harry Houdini	magician; the most famous escape artist ever
Harlan Ellison	science-fiction writer
Dustin Hoffman	actor
Modigliani	artist
Roseanne Barr	actor and a Jewish mother
Judith Resnik	astronaut

Frida Kahlo	Mexican artist
Ayn Rand	writer
Neve Campbell	actress
Frank Gehry	architect, designer of Guggenheim Museum Bilbao
Bugsy Siegel	Brooklyn-born gangster; known as the founder of Las Vegas
Harrison Ford	actor
Judy Blume	writer
Marc Chagall	painter, graphic designer
Dutch Schultz	Prohibition-era mobster; killed by Murder, Incorporated. (His real name was Arthur Flegenheimer.) His Jewish mother isn't bragging.
Jerry Seinfeld	actor

Roseanne

The woman now known simply as "Roseanne" was named Rose-anne Cherrie Barr when she was born in 1952. Her working-class Jewish family settled in Salt Lake City, which made her an auto-matic outsider. She characterized her Jewish upbringing this way: "Friday, Saturday, and Sunday morning I was a Jew; Sunday after-noon, Tuesday afternoon, and Wednesday afternoon we were Mormons." Roseanne is a Jewish mother four times over.

Jewish Inventors

Whom do we have to thank for the remote control, the Corvette, and the flexi-straw? Tip your hat to the children of Jewish mothers, ladies and gentlemen. Jews are especially well represented in the sciences, no doubt because their doting Jewish mothers encourage education—but more on that in later chapters. In the meantime, here's a list of famous Jewish inventors. Thank them the next time you play with your Barbie dolls, slip on your blue jeans, or get LASIK eye surgery—and so much more.

Famous Jewish Inventors and Their Inventions

Inventor	Invention
Robert Adler	remote control
Zora Arkus-Duntov	Corvette (codesigner)
Joseph Friedman	flexi-straw
Ruth Handler	Barbie dolls
Levi Strauss	blue jeans
Samuel Blum	LASIK eye surgery (co-inventor)
Sylvan Goldman	shopping cart
Emile Berliner	gramophone
Edwin Land	Polaroid camera
Hilda Miller	first sports bra (co-inventor)
Selman Waksman	streptomycin

Baruch Blumberg and Irving Millman	vaccine for Hepatitis B
Carl Djerassi	oral contraceptive, antihistamines
Joel Davidson	100 percent solar-powered vehicle
Gertrude Elion	anti-leukemia drugs
Peter Carl Goldmark	long-playing vinyl record
Theodore Maiman	co-inventor of the laser
David Schwartz	invented the Zeppelin

Barbie Doll

The Barbie doll, invented by Ruth Handler, debuted in 1959. Handler stated that she felt it was "important to a little girl's self-esteem to play with a doll that [had] breasts," believing it would allow girls to imagine their future as adult women. However, a woman with Barbie's body would be 7 feet, 2 inches tall; weigh 115 pounds; and measure 48-18-30. I should be so lucky.

Jewish Mothers Who Also Write (When They're Not Worrying about Their Children)

Aside from yours truly, many Jewish mothers have distinguished themselves in print. One of my favorites is the late Wendy Wasserstein, an award-winning playwright.

Describing herself, Wasserstein said, "My father loved me dearly, but I'm not a Jewish American Princess. I'm a Jewish mother, but I'm not Molly Goldberg." (You'll read about Molly Goldberg later.)

Wendy Wasserstein

A true "Noo Yawker," Wasserstein was born in Brooklyn in 1950. Her family is quite accomplished: Her grandfather Simon Shliefer was a scholar and a playwright. He immigrated to America from Poland. Once in America, he became a Hebrew school principal. Wendy's brother Bruce is a giant in the investment industry. Wasserstein herself was an outstanding scholar, earning her undergraduate degree in history from Mount Holyoke College in 1971 and her Masters in Fine Art from the Yale School of Drama five years later. Wasserstein, who never married, once said that her parents allowed her to attend Yale in the hope that she would meet a suitable Jewish man, perferably an attorney, and settle down to produce grandchildren for them.

In 1977, Wasserstein sprang to the critics' attention with her play *Uncommon Women and Others*. The play had a stellar cast, including Glenn Close, Swoosie Kurtz, and Jill Eikenberry. PBS later produced the play as a TV special, replacing Close with Meryl Streep.

Erica Jong

Born in 1942, Jong is likely most famous for *Fear of Flying* (1973), which created a sensation for its frank treatment of women's sexuality. Hey, Jewish Mamas can be hot, too.

Posssessed of prodigious talent, Wasserstein soon carved out a niche for herself with plays about bright, successful women. Her plays included *The Sisters Rosensweig, Isn't It Romantic, An American Daughter, Old Money*, and *Third*. Wasserstein's talent was publicly acknowledged in 1989 when her play *The Heidi Chronicles* was awarded both the Tony and the Pulitzer Prize. Wasserstein herself viewed her plays as "political acts," probing the inner lives of bright and thoughtful women who are torn between traditional expectations and modern careers. Sounds like the stereotype of the Jewish mother, eh?

Three years after her Broadway triumph, Wasserstein gave birth to her dauhter, Lucy Jane. The conception and birth had been marked by challenges, which Wasserstein described in her book *Shiksa Goddess (Or How I Spent My Forties)*. Tragically, Wasserstein's life was cut short in 2006, when she died of lymphoma. Broadway's lights were dimmed in tribute the night after her passing.

Other Notable Female Jewish Writers

Jewish Writer	Claim to Fame
Hannah Arendt	chronicler of ethics, or the lack thereof
Aimee Bender	novelist and short-story writer
Hortense Calisher	novelist
Allegra Goodman	novelist
Rona Jaffe	novelist
Erica Jong	novelist
Judith Krantz	novelist
Fran Lebowitz	sardonic social commentator
Tillie Olsen	short-story writer
Ayn Rand	rugged individualism
Barbara Rogan	novelist

The Portable Jewish Mother

Susan Sontag	essayist and novelist
Gertrude Stein	novelist and social connector
Jacqueline Susann	novelist

In Chapter 3, you'll explore the stereotype of the Jewish mother.

Enter the Jewish Mother

Two Jewish women
are speaking about their sons
in state prison. The first says: "Oy!
My son has it so hard locked away in
maximum security. He never sees the light of
day and has a horrible life." The second says:
"My son is in minimum security. He exercises
every day, he spends time in the prison library,
and writes home each week." "Oy!" says
the first woman, "You must get such
naches [joy] from your son."

A haiku is a seventeen-syllable verse form, arranged in three lines of five, seven, and five syllables. It's a traditional Japanese verse form, but some jokester applied it to Jewish mothers as well. Here's my favorite Jewish mother haiku:

Testing the warm milk
on her wrist, she beams—nice, but
her son is forty.

Actors get typecast all the time, but no one has gotten as completely typecast as the Jewish mother. Whether we call her a "Jewish mother," a "Yiddishe mama," or "Happy Surprise" (as my daughter-in-law calls me), the result is the same: the Jewish mother stereotype. It's not unique to America, either; Jewish mother poster girls can be found around the globe. Let me prove it to you. Take the following quiz to see how much you know about this familiar international stereotype. You might be surprised at your level of expertise.

Jewish Mothers Span the World

Only two of the following historical figures really had Jewish mothers, but we realize that not everyone can be so lucky to be born of a Yiddishe Mama. Try matching each Jewish mother with her comment.

My Son, the Explorer

1 **Mona Lisa's** Jewish mother

2 **Christopher Columbus's** Jewish mother

3 **Michelangelo's** Jewish mother

4 **Napoleon's** Jewish mother

5 **Abraham Lincoln's** Jewish mother

6 **George Washington's** Jewish mother

7 **Thomas Edison's** Jewish mother

8 **Paul Revere's** Jewish mother

9 **Albert Einstein's** Jewish mother

10 **Moses'** Jewish mother

The Portable Jewish Mother

___ "You want maybe to put a knife through your mother's heart? Try crossing the Delaware again in the middle of winter without your galoshes and muffler."

___ "Again with the foolish hat! Why can't you wear a baseball cap like the other kids?"

___ "But it's your senior photograph! Couldn't you have done something about your hair?"

___ "That's a likely story. Now tell me where you've *really* been for the last forty years."

___ "Why can't you paint on walls like other children? Do you know how hard it is to get paint off the ceiling?"

___ "This you call a smile, after all the money your father and I spent on braces?"

___ "All right, if you're not hiding your report card inside your jacket, take your hand out of there and show me!"

___ "Of course I'm proud that you invented the electric light bulb. Now turn it off and go to sleep. You have school tomorrow and you know the SATs are coming up."

___ "I don't care what you've discovered; still you never write, you never call."

___ "You're not going anywhere, young man. Midnight is long past your curfew and you have a math test tomorrow."

Answers

6 **Washington's** Jewish mother

"You want maybe to put a knife through your mother's heart? Try crossing the Delaware again in the middle of winter without your galoshes and muffler."

5 **Abraham Lincoln's** Jewish mother

"Again with the foolish hat! Why can't you wear a baseball cap like the other kids?"

9 **Albert Einstein's** Jewish mother

"But it's your senior photograph! Couldn't you have done something about your hair?"

10 **Moses' Jewish** mother

"That's a likely story. Now tell me where you've really been for the last forty years."

3 **Michelangelo's** Jewish mother

"Why can't you paint on walls like other children? Do you know how hard it is to get paint off the ceiling?"

1 **Mona Lisa's** Jewish mother

"This you call a smile, after all the money your father and I spent on braces?"

4 **Napoleon's** Jewish mother

"All right, if you're not hiding your report card inside your jacket, take your hand out of there and show me!"

7 **Thomas Edison's** Jewish mother

"Of course I'm proud that you invented the electric light bulb. Now turn it off and go to sleep. You have school tomorrow and you know the SATs are coming up."

2 **Christopher Columbus's** Jewish mother

"I don't care what you've discovered; still you never write, you never call."

8 **Paul Revere's** Jewish mother

"You're not going anywhere, young man. Midnight is long past your curfew and you have a math test tomorrow."

And who were the two lucky boys
to be born of Jewish mothers?

Albert Einstein and **Moses**, natch.

Mein Yiddishe Mama

"Mein Yiddishe Mama" ("My Jewish Mother") is a classic sentimental 1925 Yiddish song. Jack Yellen wrote the tune; Lew Pol-
lack and Yellen, the lyrics. The song, as with so many like it,
idealized the Jewish mother.

The Stereotype of the Jewish Mother

Q: *What's the difference between a rottweiler and
a Jewish mother?*

A: *Eventually, the rottweiler lets go.*

There are black mothers, Italian mothers, Polish mothers, and
WASP mothers (as well as many more types of mothers), but
only Jewish mothers have their own stereotype. Perhaps we can
blame their sons, those Catskill comedians who mocked their
mammas while they loved them so fiercely. The media must
share some of the blame, especially that archvillain: television.
Regardless of the cause, Jewish mothers are supposed to fit into a
neat mold. They rarely do, but that hasn't had any impact on the
longevity and strength of the stereotype.

Benevolent

In the 1940s and 1950s, the media portrayed the Jewish mother as a kindly busybody who solved nearly all problems through common sense and kindness. She was personified by Gertrude Berg, the creator, primary writer, and star of her own weekly situation comedy, *The Goldbergs*. When the show made the transition from radio to television, Berg was already thoroughly identified in the public mind with her lifelong dramatic persona, Molly Goldberg, a Jewish-American mother she had developed into a sweetly quintessential stereotype.

The Borscht Belt

Many famous comedians got their start in the "Borscht Belt," the nickname for the summer resorts in the Catskill Mountains popular with Jewish families in the 1930s, 1940s, and 1950s. The headliners included Woody Allen, Morey Amsterdam, Milton Berle, Mel Brooks, Lenny Bruce, George Burns, Red Buttons, Sid Caesar, Rodney Dangerfield, Phyllis Diller, Buddy Hackett, Mickey Katz (father of Joel Grey), Danny Kaye, Jerry Lewis, Jackie Mason, Carl Reiner, Don Rickles, Joan Rivers, and Jonathan Winters. Jewish mothers didn't stand a chance against this high-powered comedic lineup.

Berg drew her character from the lives of Eastern European Jews who lived in small villages called *shtetls*. The Jewish mother was the family's backbone, the giver of unconditional love and support. She was always available to listen, comfort, assist, and feed. She sacrificed so her children could have what they needed. Generous, altruistic, and dependable, she helped protect the family from the very real threat of pogroms. She's clever, personable, and intelligent, too. In short, Berg's Jewish mother was an ideal and idealized character, what everyone wants in a mother.

Sunrise, Sunset

Fiddler on the Roof remains the best glimpse of life in the Russian shtetls. The musical opened on Broadway in 1964 with Zero Mostel in the lead role of Tevye the milkman. His wife Golde was played by Maria Karnilova; Yente the matchmaker was played by Beatrice Arthur. Both Golde and Yente are archetypal Jewish mothers. The play is loosely based on the stories of Tevye the Milkman by the Russian-Jewish writer Sholom Aleichem, originally published in 1949. The play has been revived many times and was made into a successful movie.

The following joke sums up the benevolent Jewish mother:

The other day, Sylvia's telephone rings at 8:30 in the morning. The minute she picks it up she hears, "Oy! Ma! Help! I need you! Both the kids have the measles and are crying upstairs. The Hadassah ladies are due at the house for lunch and the Frigidaire is broken and everything I made last night is spoiled. The car broke down so I can't even go to the supermarket! What am I going to do?"

"Don't worry, darling," Sylvia tells her. "You call the repairman. In the meantime, I'll take the bus to the Long Island Railroad, and come out to your house. I'll walk the two miles from the station. On the way, I'll stop off at Walbaum's and pick up a few things for lunch. I'll take care of the kids. Then I'll cook a nice lunch for the Hadassah ladies. I'll even make dinner for Barry."

"Who's Barry?" she asks.

"Barry . . . your husband. The lawyer," Sylvia says.

She says, "But, Ma, my husband is David. Is this 353-3889?"

"No," says Sylvia, "this is 353-3886."

There is a groan on the other end of the line. "Oy!! Does this mean you're not coming?"

Bitchy

By the 1970s, however, the helpful Jewish mama had become the purveyor of unending guilt. She demanded loyalty and became a "problem." Molly Goldberg's kind mothering on *The Goldbergs* had become Sylvia Fine's shrill nagging on *The Nanny*. According to the way Jewish mothers were now portrayed on television, Jewish children were no longer *spending time* with their mothers; now they were *doing time* with them.

By the time the '90s came around, the Jewish mother had slid into caricature as materialistic, whining, and vulgar. The Jewish mother now seemed to exist solely to harass their daughters into marriage, their sons into professional careers. Neurotically overprotective, they make life miserable for everyone. They're one-dimensional, pushy, controlling, high-maintenance, shallow, and domineering. They have high, nasal voices and New York "accents." The stereotype had also come to stand for all overbearing mothers of any nationality or religion.

Come Fly with Me

The new term for an overbearing mother is the "Helicopter Mom." These are nosy mothers who are always hovering around their children and are quick to offer a teacher unwanted help. The term and the behavior it describes are not restricted to Jewish mothers.

The Portable Jewish Mother

What Makes a Jewish Mother?

Take the following quiz to see how much you know about the Jewish mother stereotype. Put a check next to each characteristic that describes a stereotypical Jewish mother.

○ 1. She's a nag. She nags morning, noon, and night. Fortunately, she's an equal-opportunity nag, nagging her children, their friends, and their friends' friends. She nags her husband, the paper boy, and even the electrician.

○ 2. She never nags. Meek and mild, she lets her children and husband walk all over her. People often take advantage of her. They consider her a doormat.

○ 3. She's overprotective of her children, especially when it comes to matters of education and health. If she thinks someone is harming her child, she'll rip them to shreds.

○ 4. She's not overprotective at all—just the opposite. She has a laissez-faire attitude toward child rearing. For instance, she'd sooner poke herself in the eye with a fork than call the school about a problem that her child is having. It's usually all the kid's fault anyway.

○ 5. She's intrusive, believing that a closed door really means "Everyone stay out but my beloved mother."

○ 6. She's not intrusive. She knocks before entering her child's room—even if the door is open.

7. She lives solely for her children. She takes extreme pride in her children's achievements and brags about her children to others.

8. She doesn't live for her children. She feels that it would be impolite to call attention to her children, so she rarely speaks about them to others. She finds fulfillment in her sewing, gardening club, and long-haul trucking.

9. She rules the roost with an iron fist; there's no doubt that she's in charge. She dominates her husband, rarely letting him speak or express an opinion.

10. Hubby rules the roost. She is the Little Woman echoing his opinions.

11. She values academic degrees—especially Ivy League ones—over manual labor. She wants her children to be doctors, lawyers, CPAs, and teachers. Maybe a dentist, but only if an orthodontist or periodontist. Sports are okay, if tennis, swimming, or golf. No contact sports, please.

12. She values manual labor over academic degrees because she wants her children to have secure union jobs as plumbers, electricians, and welders. She believes in the value of organized sports, too, especially ice hockey, football, and lacrosse.

13. She demands (and schemes, if necessary) that her children marry and reproduce.

14. She doesn't demand that her children marry. In fact, she has little interest in grandchildren because she doesn't want to baby-sit. She's too busy playing tennis.

15. She constantly fears that her children will be injured and so tries to prevent them from doing anything that she perceives as dangerous.

16. She enrolls her children in high-intensity sports, including surfing and skydiving.

17. She demands that her children obey her, often manipulating them through guilt.

18. She is standoffish, even icy cold, sipping martinis all day at the kitchen sink as she leafs through her *Better Homes and Horses* magazine.

Passover

Passover is the Jewish holiday that commemorates the Exodus and the Israelites' freedom from ancient Egypt. As described in the Book of Exodus, Passover marks the "birth" of the Jewish nation, as the Jews' ancestors were freed from being the pharaoh's slaves and allowed to become servants of God instead. The holiday falls between March 15 and April 30 and lasts seven days. For Jewish mothers, Passover means a lot of cleaning and cooking, as you'll learn later in this book.

Answers

All the odd-numbered choices are correct, if we buy into the stereotype.

You Could Buy Stock in It

Have you heard this joke?

And it came to pass that a Jewish man was elected to be president of the United States of America. So he calls his mother Sylvia in Queens and invites her to come down to Washington, D.C., for Passover.

She says, "I'd like to, but it's so much trouble . . . I mean, I have to get a cab to the airport, and I hate waiting on Queens Boulevard. . . . "

He replies, "Mom! I'm the president of the United States of America! You won't need a cab; I'll send a limo for you!"

To which his mother replies, "I know, but then I'll have to get my ticket at the airport, and try to get a seat on the plane, and I hate to sit in the middle . . . it's just too much trouble."

He replies, "Mom! I'm the president of the United States of America! I'll send Air Force One or another of my private jets for you."

The Portable Jewish Mother

To which she replies, "Oh, well, but then when we land, I'll have to carry my luggage through the airport, and try to get a cab . . . it's really too much trouble."

He replies, "Mom! I'm the president! I'll send a helicopter for you! You won't have to lift a finger."

She answers, "Yes, that's nice . . . but, you know, I still need a hotel room, and the rooms are so expensive, and I really don't like the rooms. . . ."

He answers, "Mom! I'm the president! You'll stay at the White House!"

She responds, "Well . . . all right . . . I guess I'll come."

The next day, she's on the phone with her friend Mildred, who says, "Hello, Sylvia. What's new?"

Sylvia replies: "I'm visiting my son for Passover."

Mildred says, "The doctor?"

Sylvia replies, "No . . . the other one."

As this joke shows, today's Jewish mother is a "stock character," a fictional creation that becomes instantly recognizable because it is a caricature. Naturally, this leads to jokes and parody. The jokes usually mock the overprotectiveness of the Jewish mother, her constant worry over her children, and her use of guilt to manipulate. Jewish mothers take pride in their children's professional success (but only in certain careers!) and are reputed to be domineering. We see these stereotypes in many of the jokes that make the rounds. Here are some typical samples:

The Jewish mother's overprotectiveness:
To practice Zen and the art of Jewish motorcycle maintenance, do the following: Get rid of the motorcycle. What *were* you thinking?

The Jewish mother's constant worry over her children:
At the beach Mrs. Schwartz began yelling at the lifeguard who had just pulled her daughter out of the ocean. The lifeguard says, "I'll start giving the child artificial respiration right away."

"You'll either give my Marcia real respiration or nothing!" Mrs. Schwartz demands.

The Jewish mother's use of guilt to bend others to her iron will:
A Jewish Mother's Answering Machine:
If you want chicken soup, press 1;
If you want matzoh balls with the soup, press 2;
If you want stuffed cabbage, dial 3;
If you want a piece of sponge cake, press 4;
If you want to know how am I feeling, you are calling the wrong number since nobody ever asks me how I am feeling.

The Jewish mother's excessive pride in her children's professional success:

An old Jewish woman is standing by the riverbank.

> She shouts out: "Help, help!"
>
> A passerby says: "What's the problem?"
>
> She explains: "My son the lawyer is drowning."

The Jewish mother's domineering approach:

Jewish mother: "Wake up, David! You've got to go to school!"

> David: "I don't wanna."
>
> Jewish mother: "No, you have to."
>
> David: "Gimme one reason that I have to go to school."
>
> Jewish mother: "Because you are fifty-two years old and the principal."

Portnoy's Complaint

Portnoy's Complaint, Philip Roth's seminal 1969 novel about sexual frustration, centers on the Jewish-American experience. In between kvetching about his sexual issues, the narrator explores the advantages and disadvantages of being the son of a Jewish family. Most critics accept that the novel is highly autobiographical. To this we say, "Oy! His mother deserves such thanks for all her hard work?"

Some scholars see the tradition of the strong Jewish mother as the result of the traditional Jewish philosophy of the man running the outside world of business and politics while the woman runs the inside world of family and household. We'll leave the decoding of the Jewish mother to the next chapter.

In the next chapter, you'll survey Jewish mothers through the ages to see how this stereotype developed.

Jewish Mothers Through the Ages

In 1654, 300 Dutch Jews, fed up with anti-Semitism in their hometown, set sail. Figuring, "Why not at least go to a nice place?" they landed in beautiful Barbados. Setting down their bags in Bridgetown, they built a synagogue. Destroyed by a hurricane in 1831, it has since been rebuilt several times. Not much gets us down.

Jewish mothers are everywhere. First, you've got your real Jewish mothers. There's your mother, my mother, and all those women in Hadassah. Then there's Joan Rivers, Jewish mother to an industry (entertainment, not plastic surgery). And we mustn't forget Woody Allen, a Jewish mother in trousers. Such a nebbish, but he did refine Jewish neurosis to an art form that serves as a model to Jewish sons all over the world. But now, let's start with the first Jewish mothers, the ones who set the pace for the rest of us.

The Original Jewish Mother

According to the New Testament of the Bible, Mary (Miriam) was the mother of Jesus of Nazareth. Since Jesus was unquestionably a Jew, Mary was the first Jewish mother. And if you doubt me, here are the four theological proofs that Jesus was Jewish:

* He lived at home until he was thirty.
* He went into his father's business.
* He believed his mother was still a virgin.
* His mother thought he was God.

Jesus Hailed from the West Coast

We can make an equally good case that Jesus was from California:

* He never cut his hair.
* He walked around barefoot.
* He invented a new religion.

Biblical Jewish Mothers

There's no shortage of Jewish mothers in the Old Testament, but the most famous are the four Matriarchs, known as the "mothers" in Hebrew. Featured in the Book of Genesis, these women are considered to be the ancestral "mothers" of the Jewish people. They are Sarah, Rebekah, Leah, and Rachel. They serve as role models for different facets of the Jewish mother's character and behavior.

Sarah

When God told Abraham to journey to an unknown land, Sarah accompanied him. However, when they arrived they were met with a famine, and decided to take refuge in Egypt. Fearing that Sarah's beauty would put his life in danger if their true relationship became known, Abraham passed her off as his sister.

As Abraham had feared, Pharaoh took Sarah. What goes around, comes around, and God struck Pharaoh with severe plagues, after which Pharaoh put the finger on Abraham, censured him, and kicked the couple out. But, impressed with Abraham's righteousness, Pharaoh sent his own daughter Hagar to be a handmaiden to Sarah.

When Sarah failed to conceive, she offered Hagar to Abraham as a concubine. Hagar became pregnant immediately, and began to despise her mistress. Sarah treated Hagar harshly and the Egyptian fled to the desert. There, an angel told her she would bear many children and urged her to return to her mistress. After Hagar returned, she bore Abraham a son, whom he named Ishmael.

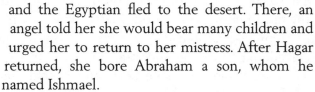

Then God sent three angels disguised as men to inform the couple of the impending birth of Isaac. Sarah was ninety years old at the time; Abraham, 100.

Rebekah

This is one of the classic stories of the Bible. In fact, it is the prototype of an ideal Jewish marriage. Initially, Rebekah glimpsed her husband-to-be while he was in a meadow praying. As a modest, well-raised young lady, she hid her face with her veil and dismounted from her camel so she would not be seen. In no haste to marry off their daughter to a stranger, Rebekah's family made Isaac stay with them for a while so their daughter could prepare for her new life. Astonishingly for the time and place, Rebekah's family asked Rebekah to agree to the marriage—which she did. Isaac then introduced her to Jewish laws and customs, married her, and loved her.

Traditional Jewish Marriage Blessing

When Rebekah's family sends her away to marry Isaac, they offer a blessing that is still bestowed on brides in religious Jewish weddings today: "Our sister, may you come to be thousands of myriads, and may your offspring inherit the gate of their enemies." (Genesis 24:60)

After two decades of marriage, Rebekah conceived the twins Esau and Jacob. However, a terrible famine descended on the land and the family fled for Gerar. To protect his beautiful wife, Isaac resorted to the subterfuge of telling everyone that she was his sister, not his spouse. This was a trick that Isaac had learned from his father Abraham.

Rachel and Leah

Leah was the first wife of the Hebrew patriarch Jacob and mother of six of the Twelve Tribes of Israel. She became Jacob's wife through a deception on the part of her father.

Jacob left home to avoid being killed by his brother Esau and possibly to find a wife. By a well, he encountered Rachel and decided to marry her.

For seven years, Jacob toiled for Laban, Rachel's father, in exchange for being allowed to marry Rachel. Then came the old switcheroo: Laban switched Leah for Rachel. Jacob wanted Rachel, so he promised to work another seven years for Laban. And he got her.

Jacob loved Rachel more than Leah, so God enabled Leah to bear four sons in quick succession. Since she could not conceive, Rachel offered her handmaid Bilhah as Jacob's third wife. He accepted, and Rachel raised the two sons that Bilhah bore. Leah responded by offering her handmaid Zilpah as Jacob's fourth wife, and Leah raised the two sons that Zilpah bore. Leah bore three more children; Rachel had two sons.

Contemporary Jewish Mothers

Now let's look at contemporary Jewish mothers. The archetypal Jewish mother is Golda Meir, legendary mother to the Jewish state as well as her own two children. A superhuman woman, she's one of my personal heroes.

Golda Meir

Golda Meir (1898–1978) served as the minister of labor, foreign minister, and then as the fourth prime minister of Israel from 1969 to 1974. To say that she was a strong lady would be an understatement: David Ben-Gurion once described her as "the only man in the Cabinet."

Born Golda Mabovitz to a very poor family in Russia, she immigrated to America when she was eight years old, settling in Wisconsin with her family. Even though just a child, she often ran the family's grocery store alone when her parents went to restock. Despite not knowing any English when she arrived in America, Golda graduated as valedictorian of her high school class.

As a teenager, Golda became a fervent Zionist. She married Morris Myerson in 1917 and the couple immigrated to Palestine four years later. They joined a kibbutz (a cooperative farm), where Golda quickly emerged as a natural leader. When her husband tired of farm life, they left the kibbutz, had two children, and Golda continued moving up the political ladder. The marriage dissolved under the demands of Golda's increasingly public life, but the couple never formally divorced.

In 1948, Golda was a signer of the Declaration of Establishment of Israel. Here's how she described the moment: "After I signed, I cried. When I studied American history as a schoolgirl and I read about those who signed the Declaration of Independence, I couldn't imagine these were real people doing something real. And there I was sitting down and signing a declaration of establishment."

She continued to ascend the ranks of the new government, serving as Israel's first ambassador to the Soviet Union. When she assumed the role of Israeli minister of labor in 1949, Golda Hebraicized her last name to *Meir*, which means "makes a light." In 1969, the government chose Golda to become prime minister after Levi Eshkol's death.

Meir came out of retirement to assume the office. She served continuously in the Knesset (Israeli Parliament) until 1974. She was prime minister during the 1973 Yom Kippur War. She had helped establish a state, define it, and defend it. She's a role model for all women, but especially strong Jewish mothers.

Dear Abby and Ann Landers, Too

Identical twin advice columnists Ann Landers and Dear Abby were authentic Jewish mothers. Ann Landers's real name was Esther Pauline Friedman Lederer; Dear Abby's name was Pauline Esther Friedman Phillips. (Not a very imaginative family, eh?) Pauline was seventeen minutes younger than Esther, if you care. They grew up in Sioux City, Iowa, the daughters of Russian-Jewish immigrants.

Esther, nicknamed "Eppie" (1918–2002), toiled at her keyboard as Ann Landers for nearly fifty years, doling out astringent but solid advice. She won a contest to take over the column in 1955, and wound up as owner of the copyright. The column died with her.

Pauline (1918–), nicknamed "Popo," wrote her column as Abigail Van Buren. Although the twins were very close as children and young adults—they even had a joint wedding ceremony in 1939—they grew apart over professional competition. The twins publicly reconciled in 1964, although some suggest the tiff lasted after death. Knowing Jewish families firsthand, this wouldn't surprise me at all.

But still these two women raised families, built empires, and improved lives. For half a century, they gave advice to one and all. Perhaps even more important, they stood up against injustice. Ann in particular spoke out against anti-Semitism and racism.

Her column ran in more than 1,000 newspapers and was translated into more than twenty languages. She reached millions and millions of readers, in effect making her America's Mother. As with Golda Meir, both Ann Landers and Dear Abby are Jewish mamas who could serve as superb role models for all women.

Jewish Mother Wannabes

Here, the prototype is Madonna, who has embraced Jewish mysticism and dropped that pesky Italian last name. She may have been born a shiksa (non-Jewish girl), but she's got chutzpah (nerve). Anne Meara became a Jewish mother when she married Jerry Stiller and gave birth to Ben Stiller; Courtney Love is Jewish, but she's such a meshuggeneh (crazy person), that we'll put her on the bottom of the list. Fortunately, we have enough great real Jewish mothers that we don't have to deal with the wonky ones.

In the next chapters, we'll identify some fictional Jewish mothers and explore some more myths and misconceptions about the Jewish mother. We'll also see if we can decode the stereotype and get to the truth.

CHAPTER 5

Some Jewish Mothers

Wonder What Portnoy Had to Complain About

Selma and Esther meet after fifty years. Selma says: "My son the doctor has four great kids. My daughter the lawyer has three great kids. So, Esther, how about your kids?" Esther replies, "Unfortunately, Mel and I don't have any children so we don't have any grandchildren either." Selma says, "No children? . . . and no grandkids? So tell me, Esther, what do you do for aggravation?"

God could not be everywhere, so He invented Jewish mothers.
—Old Jewish Proverb

All Mothers Are Jewish Mothers

In 1969, a reporter interviewed a number of Jewish mothers about how the culture tends to perceive them as nagging, guilt-inducing, overprotective shrews. Among the women she interviewed was Philip Roth's mother. Remember, as mentioned in Chapter 3, Philip Roth is the author of the novel *Portnoy's Complaint*, an extended whine about his mother, being Jewish, and sexual issues. Mama Roth's comment? "I think all mothers are Jewish mothers."

Proof #1: Love Me Tender

Elvis Presley slept in the same bed with his mother Gladys until he reached puberty. Until Elvis entered high school, she walked him back and forth to school every day and made him take along his own silverware so that he wouldn't catch germs from the other kids at lunch. Gladys forbade young Elvis from going swimming or doing anything that might put him in danger. The two of them also conversed in their own baby talk that only they could understand. The Jewish mother's fabled overprotectiveness is *nothing* compared to Elvis and his Mama.

70

Proof #2: Going Batty

The mother of a Mexican free-tailed bat finds and nurses her own young, even in huge colonies where many millions of babies cluster at up to 500 bats per square foot. And we think that Jewish mothers are obsessed with food.

Proof #3: It's a Beautiful Day in This Neighborhood

Many of the sweaters worn by Mr. Rogers on the popular television show *Mr. Rogers' Neighborhood* were actually knitted by his real mother. With her own two hands. Such a Jewish-mother thing to do, but Mrs. Rogers wasn't Jewish.

Proof #4: Average Fourth Graders

Remember that Jewish mothers are reputed to boss their husbands and children mercilessly. Some average nine-year-olds were asked, "Who's the boss at your house?" Here's what they said:

1. Mom doesn't want to be boss, but she has to because dad's such a goofball.
2. Mom. You can tell by room inspection. She sees the stuff under the bed.
3. I guess Mom is, but only because she has a lot more to do than dad.

But we know that a Jewish mother is like any other good mother: concerned about her children, her husband, her family, and herself. All good mothers are Jewish mothers at heart. That hasn't affected the Jewish mother stereotype, however. In this chapter, we'll discover more myths and misconceptions about Jewish mothers.

Start with a quick quiz. See if you can identify the Jewish mothers on the following list. Here's a clue: Half the women are Jewish mothers and half are not.

Real Jewish Mothers or Fake Jewish Mothers?

Take the following quiz to see if you can identify the real Jewish mothers scattered among the imposters. Put a check mark next to the name of each person you think is an authentic Jewish mother.

○ 1. Madeleine Albright
○ 2. Mother Teresa
○ 3. Ruth Bader Ginsburg
○ 4. Patty Duke
○ 5. Paula Abdul
○ 6. Mia Farrow
○ 7. Phoebe Cates
○ 8. Melissa Joan Hart
○ 9. Melissa Gilbert
○ 10. Whistler's Mother

○ 11. Kyra Sedgwick
○ 12. Rosie O'Donnell
○ 13. Debra Winger
○ 14. Brooke Shields
○ 15. Bette Midler
○ 16. Marge Simpson
○ 17. Dinah Shore
○ 18. Whoopi Goldberg
○ 19. Barbara Walters
○ 20. Angelina Jolie

Answers

All the odd numbers are real Jewish mothers; all the even numbers are goyim. And there's no symbolism in the fact that I assigned the odd numbers to the Jewish mothers.

Jewish Mother Face-Off

1. **Madeleine Albright** According to Jewish law, she's Jewish. Former secretary of state under President Clinton, Albright was born Marie Jana Korbelova in Czechoslovakia and raised Roman Catholic in England. Her parents were Catholic converts from Judaism, which she claims she never knew. She has children, so she's a Jewish mother.
2. **Mother Teresa** Need I say more? Nuns are rarely Jewish and usually don't have children.
3. **Ruth Bader Ginsburg** The Supreme Court Justice is Jewish. She and her husband Martin have a daughter, Jane, and a son, James. Thus, she is a Jewish mother.
4. **Patty Duke** Not a Jew, but a fine actress nonetheless.
5. **Paula Abdul** Of Jewish heritage on both sides: her father is a Sephardic Jew and her mother is an Ashkenazi Jew. Thus, she is a Jewish mother. Nonetheless, people often think she's African-American. They're wrong.
6. **Mia Farrow** Mother to many and despite her long-term relationship with Woody Allen, not a Jew.

Some Jewish Mothers . . .

7. **Phoebe Cates** Jewish. Born Phoebe Belle Katz, she achieved icon status in the early 1980s for her role in the teen comedy *Fast Times at Ridgemont High*, in which she stripped off her bikini top in a slow-motion fantasy sequence. In 1984, *Harper's Bazaar* included her in their list of America's 10 Most Beautiful Women. This gorgeous Jewish mama is married to fellow actor Kevin Kline. (Kline's father was Jewish and his Irish-American mother was a Roman Catholic. Kline was raised Catholic.)

8. **Melissa Joan Hart** An Irish-American actress, and not Jewish.

9. **Melissa Gilbert** Jewish. Born in Los Angeles to a Jewish family, Gilbert was adopted by actor Paul Gilbert and his wife Barbara Crane. Although she's the mother of two sons, Gilbert is far better known for her role as the middle daughter Laura on the television series *Little House on the Prairie* (1974–1983). Nonetheless, she's a genuine Jewish mother.

10. **Whistler's Mother** Not Jewish. In 1871, Anna McNeill Whistler posed for the painting while living in England with her son James.

11. **Kyra Sedgwick** Sedgwick's father was an Episcopalian and her mother was Jewish. Kyra considers herself Jewish, as do we. She and her husband Kevin Bacon have two children, a son and a daughter. Thus, she is a Jewish mother.

12. **Rosie O'Donnell** Not Jewish; thus, not a Jewish mother.

The Portable Jewish Mother

13. **Debra Winger** Very Jewish. Born Mary Debra Winger in Cleveland to a Jewish family, Winger spent several years in Israel and served in the Israel Defense Forces before becoming an actress and a mother.

14. **Brooke Shields** Called "the whitest woman in America" by Eddie Murphy, Shields is from a very aristocratic Irish-Italian family. Through her Italian grandmother, Shields is a descendant of Lucrezia Borgia, Holy Roman Emperor Charles V, Honoré I of Monaco, and Henry IV of France. Not a Jew among them, so Brooke is not Jewish either.

15. **Bette Midler** The Divine Miss M is Jewish. Born in Hawaii, she has one daughter. Thus, she is a Jewish mother.

16. **Marge Simpson** The cartoon figure on *The Simpsons* is voiced by the Jewish actress Julie Kavner but is not Jewish herself. Her most notable physical feature is her blue hair, styled into a high beehive.

17. **Dinah Shore** She was Jewish. Born to Solomon and Anna Stein Shore, Jewish immigrants from Russia, Frances Rose Shore (1916–1994) was a singer, actress, and talk show host. She had a son, so she is a real Jewish mother.

18. **Whoopi Goldberg** Born Caryn Elaine Johnson, Whoopi's father was a Protestant preacher. She claims to be Catholic, Buddhist, and Jewish, but doesn't consider herself a member of any religion. We're classifying her a goy, despite her surname.

Some Jewish Mothers . . .

19. Barbara Walters She's Jewish. Her father was a Jewish immigrant from London; her mother, the daughter of Polish Jewish immigrants. She has a daughter, so Baba gets Jewish mother status.

20. Angelina Jolie Not Jewish. Jolie is Czech and English on her father's side, and French-Canadian and Iroquois on her mother's side.

CHAPTER 6

Mama Drama

God couldn't be all over, so he invented mothers. And just in case they screwed it up, he invented Jewish mothers to check up on everyone else. (It's raining. Don't forget your galoshes.)

Lucy, You Got Some 'Splaining to Do

A medieval Jewish folktale describes a young man who begs his mother for her heart, which his beloved has demanded as a wedding gift. Of course, his mother offers her heart without hesitation. As the young man runs to deliver the heart, he stumbles, and falls, dropping the heart to the ground. From the heart he hears the question: "Did you hurt yourself, my beloved son?"

We know the stereotype: Jewish mothers are hyper-vigilant, difficult, guilt-producing. Living vicariously through their children, they make their children feel helpless without them. They force food, academic achievement, and love. We know the myth has legs—few stereotypes are as pervasive—but why? We can't attribute the stereotype to the prevalence of Jewish mothers. After all, Jews make up only about 2 percent of the population. And less than half of that number is female.

So here are a few explanations for the omnipresence of the myth of the Jewish mother.

Religious Explanation of the Jewish Mother Stereotype

The actor Jason Alexander told his mother he was either going to regular school or Hebrew school, but not both. His mother, Ruth Greenspan, said, "I told him he had to go to both to become an educated person and to know what it means to be a Jew. He replied, "I already know—it means to suffer."

According to this theory, some Jewish men project their shame at not being gentile onto their mothers, who have by definition locked them into an eternal struggle with their identity. The stereotypical Jewish mother represents all the pain, fear, and rage these Jewish men feel as they deal with anti-Semitism and attempt to assimilate into the Christian culture. Jewish women stand for the aspects of Jewish identity that must be rejected, and so the mother must be rejected as well. The son projects onto the mother all the characteristics he hates in himself: chiefly, his Jewishness. By demonizing his mother, some of the burdens of this cultural and religious identity can be relieved.

Taking this one step further, Jewish children often do well in school because of parental support, upping the academic ante for everyone else. People drew the line from the children to their mothers: Hence, the Jewish mother must be a pushy, aggressive, carping shrew or her children wouldn't work so hard to win her approval. In this interpretation, the Jewish mother is merely another manifestation of anti-Semitism.

Mythological Explanation of the Jewish Mother Stereotype

In this explanation, we reach back to the mythological goddess Demeter, the Earth Mother and Goddess of Grain. Called Ceres in Roman mythology, Demeter possesses the ability to nurture both people and the earth. She also helps nurture marriages.

Demeter is the mother who takes care of her children, but too much care and you create the Smother Mother . . . also known as the stereotype of the Jewish mother. In trying to protect her children, the Jewish mother can become overly controlling, bossy, and shrill.

Psychological Explanation of the Jewish Mother Stereotype

Some psychologists would have us believe that the Jewish mother is a pathology, a disease. Because women are excluded from many official privileges and responsibilities in Orthodox Judaism, they must live through their sons, so this theory goes. Legal, political, and religious authority rests with men, so the Jewish mother must manipulate her husband and children in order to achieve power and status.

Sigmund Freud, the Big Daddy of Psychology, reinforced this notion, saying, "The only thing that brings a mother undiluted satisfaction is her relationship to her son; it is quite the most complete relationship between human beings."

Ironically, Freud had a long and close relationship with his mother—the essence of the classic Jewish mother-son love. She lived to be 95, dying when Freud was 74. Freud was his mother's favorite—*Mein goldener Sigi* ("My Golden Ziggy"), she called him. Freud hinted repeatedly of the power of her love, stating more than once that "if a man has been his mother's undisputed darling he retains throughout his life the triumphant feeling, the confidence in success, which seldom brings actual success with it."

Sigmund Freud

Sigmund Freud lived from 1856 to 1939. An Austrian physician, he is acknowledged as the father of the psychoanalytical school of psychology.

Freud is best known for his studies of sexual desire, repression, and the unconscious mind. His first patient was, of course, a Jewish mother.

"I found in myself a constant love for my mother, and jealousy of my father. I now consider this to be a universal event in childhood." He sought to anchor this pattern of development in the dynamics of the mind, and so an influential theory was born.

A traditional Jewish mother totally rejects this explanation, of course, because she stresses being respected and honored by her children. Hence, the classic dismissal of Freudian theory: "Oedipus shmoedipus! A boy shouldn't love his mother?"

Feminist Explanation of the Jewish Mother Stereotype

In this explanation, the Jewish mother exposes the ambiguities in motherhood. On one hand, women are subjected to tremendous social pressure to center their lives around their homes and their children. On the other hand, the children blame their mothers for this as they grow up. "Who told you to give up your life for me?" they whine. "You didn't complain as we were schlepping you to the orthodontist, soccer practice, and SAT classes," we mutter.

Queen Victoria

For her devotion to her husband, Albert, Queen Victoria was considered a model "Angel in the House." She also managed to find time to govern Great Britain, Ireland, and India for sixty-four years (1837–1901). Not Jewish, but strong enough to be a Jewish mama anyway.

Second, according to this explanation, women yearn to be mothers, but not only mothers. They want power, but how can you get power inside the domestic realm? By dominating your husband and children. The mother uses the child to give her life meaning and gain recognition and social status. Then children turn on their mothers as objects who either did too much or not enough for them. Further, when we mock women's attempts to gain power inside and outside the home by perpetuating the Jewish mother stereotype, we can keep women under control. In part, the feminist perspective is a reaction to the Victorian view of women, which is sadly still alive today.

The ideal Victorian wife/woman/mother was expected to be devoted and submissive to her husband. She was passive and powerless, meek, charming, graceful, sympathetic, self-sacrificing, pious, and above all—pure.

Believing that his wife Emily was the perfect Victorian wife, Coventry Patmore wrote a poem called "The Angel in the House" about her in 1854. Though it didn't receive much attention when it was first published in 1854, the poem became increasingly popular through the rest of the nineteenth century and continued to be influential into the twentieth century. *Really* influential. About eighty years later, Virginia Woolf tried to smash the ideal of the Angel in the House. She wrote: "Killing the Angel in the House was part of the occupation of a woman writer." The Jewish mother is the logical extension of this ideal.

Sociological Explanation of the Jewish Mother Stereotype

Good mothers are by our sides when we experience some of life's most painful moments as well as some of life's greatest joys. This makes it easy to blame mothers for everything that goes wrong, especially things that are wrong with ourselves.

The media has perpetuated the stereotype of the Jewish mother precisely because it strikes a chord with so many people of so many races, religions, and cultures. Using humor helps us deal with the difficulties of growing up and separating from our mothers, especially today when so many young adults return to the nest. Since they don't separate from their parents, these "children" battle with these feelings for much longer than many adult children did in past generations.

For instance, in spring 2003, nearly three-fifths of men aged twenty to twenty-four lived with their parents, compared with half in 1991. For women, the proportion of twenty- to twenty-four-year-olds living with their parents increased from a third to nearly two-fifths. And the numbers continue to rise. Some young people may be delaying leaving home because of economic necessity, such as difficulties entering the housing market. Others, lazy slugs, simply choose to continue living with their parents because work requires too much effort. Regardless, the longer they delay flying off on their own, the longer they grapple with their conflicting feelings of love and resentment and gratitude and anger toward their mother . . . the Jewish Mother Stereotype.

The Nest Isn't So Empty

"Empty nest syndrome" is a feeling of depression and loneliness that some parents feel when their children leave home. Since adult children don't seem to be leaving the nest anymore, many parents are missing the chance to suffer in this particular way. Jewish mothers like to keep their children close, but not this close.

Famous Fictional Jewish Mothers

Now that we've explored some of the reasons for the Jewish mother stereotype, let's see how the stereotype plays out in the media. After all, that's how the stereotype is spread. If you watch as much television as I do, completing this quiz will be easier than finding the remote control. Fill in the television show, book, or movie that features each fictional Jewish mama.

Let My People Go ... to the Movies

Name	Show, Book, or Movie
Bobbi Adler	
Armand	
Sylvia Buchman	
Estelle Costanza	
Sylvia Fine	
Mrs. Focker	
Golde	
Ida Morgenstern	
Mrs. Portnoy	
Helen Seinfeld	
Lilith Sternin	

Answers

Name	Show, Book, or Movie
Bobbi Adler	Grace's mother on the television show *Will & Grace*
Armand	Val Goldman's "mother" in the movie *The Birdcage*
Sylvia Buchman	Paul Buchman's mother on the television show *Mad About You*

86

Estelle Costanza	George's mother on the television show *Seinfeld*
Sylvia Fine	Fran's mother on the television show *The Nanny*
Mrs. Focker	Greg's mother in the movie *Meet the Fockers*
Golde	Mother of four daughters in the movie and stage play *Fiddler on the Roof*
Ida Morgenstern	Rhoda Morgenstern's mother on the television show *The Mary Tyler Moore Show*
Mrs. Portnoy	Alexander Portnoy's mother in Philip Roth's novel *Portnoy's Complaint*
Helen Seinfeld	Jerry's mother on the television show *Seinfeld*
Lilith Sternin	Frederick's mother on the television show *Frasier*

Why Did God Make Jewish Mothers?

Young kids were asked just this question. From the mouths of babes, the saying goes, and here are their answers:

Why did God make mothers?

1. She's the only one who knows where the Scotch tape is.
2. Mostly to clean the house.
3. To help us out of there when we were getting born.

Why did God give you your mother and not some other mom?
1. We're related.
2. God knew she likes me a lot more than other people's moms like me.

What's the difference between moms and dads?
1. Dads are taller and stronger, but moms have all the real power because that's who you got to ask if you want to sleep over at your friend's house.
2. Moms know how to talk to teachers without scaring them.
3. Moms have magic; they make you feel better without medicine.

Famous Sayings by Jewish Mothers in the Bible

Samson (or Shimshon), a good Jewish boy, is the third to last of the Judges of the ancient Children of Israel mentioned in the Bible. A Herculean figure, Samson used his enormous strength to fight his enemies and perform heroic feats unachievable by ordinary men. These include wrestling a lion, slaying an entire army with nothing more than a donkey's jawbone, and tearing down an entire building. No doubt his mother said, "Samson! Get your hand out of that lion. You don't know where it's been!"

Seriously, his most important feat, of course, is killing many Philistines in one stunning stroke, sacrificing his life in the process.

After many adventures, Samson fell in love with Delilah. The Philistines ask her for the secret of Samson's strength, which, Samson had revealed to Delilah, is his hair. Delilah has a servant shave Samson's seven locks. Since that breaks the Nazarite oath, Samson is captured by the Philistines, who gouge out his eyes. Samson is brought to Gaza, imprisoned, and forced to grind grain.

Strong Man

The definitive film version of the Biblical Samson is, of course, the 1949 Cecil B. DeMille film *Samson and Delilah*, starring Victor Mature as Samson. The son of a German-Swiss couple, Mature wasn't fortunate enough to have a Jewish mother.

One day when all the Philistines are gathered in the temple, Samson prays to God to allow him to revenge the loss of his sight, saying: "Let me die with the Philistines!" The temple falls, crushing the Philistines. The text reads: "Thus he killed many more as he died than while he lived."

Here's what some other Jewish mothers from the Bible said:

* **David's mother:** "David! I told you not to play in the house with that sling! Go practice your harp. We pay good money for those lessons."
* **Abraham's mother:** "Abraham! Stop wandering around the countryside and get home for supper."
* **Cain's mother:** "Cain! Get off your brother! You're going to kill him some day."
* **Noah's mother:** "Noah! No, you can't keep them. I told you—don't bring home any more strays."
* **Jesus' mother:** "Jesus, close the door! What do you think; you were born in a barn?"

CHAPTER 7

Basic Training:

Jewish Mothers Are Made, Not Born

Miriam Schwartz is having a very hard time with her teenage son, so she takes him to see a psychoanalyst. After several sessions, the doctor calls Miriam into his office and says, "Your son has an Oedipus complex." "Oedipus Shmedipus," answers Miriam, "As long as he loves his mother." In this chapter, you'll explore the Jewish mother stereotype in more detail.

An elderly Jewish man lay dying in his bed. In death's agony, he suddenly smelled the aroma of his favorite rugelach wafting up the stairs. He gathered his remaining strength and lifted himself from the bed.

Leaning against the wall, he slowly made his way out of the bedroom and, with even greater effort, forced himself down the stairs, gripping the railing with both hands. With labored breath, he leaned against the door frame, gazing into the kitchen.

Were it not for death's agony, he would have thought himself already in heaven.

There, spread out on paper towels on the kitchen table were literally hundreds of his favorite rugelach. Was it heaven? Or was it one final act of love from his devoted wife, seeing to it that he left this world a happy man?

Mustering one great final effort, he threw himself toward the table, landing on his knees in a heap. His lips parted: The wondrous taste of the pastry was almost in his mouth, bringing him back to life.

Trembling, the aged and withered hand made its way to a piece of rugelach at the edge of the table. Suddenly, his hand was smacked with a spatula.

"Stay out of those," said his wife, holding the spatula. "They're for the after."

The Portable Jewish Mother

Rugelach

Rugelach is a Jewish pastry of Ashkenazic origin. These delicious cookies are often made with a rich cream cheese dough and filled with raisins, walnuts, cinnamon, chocolate, or apricot preserves. Although they are small—usually no more than two inches each—they're very fattening but worth every calorie. Smart Jewish mothers buy them because they're too much work to make.

I brought a bag of rugelach with me into the labor room during the birth of child #1. (Hey, they don't call it labor for nothing.) The doctor ate them all. He's a superb doctor, but when I had my second child, I went to another obstetrician. Hey, the doctor had eaten all the rugelach. As a Jewish mother, I know well that some things are unforgivable.

Clearly, starting out being Jewish and becoming a mother gives you a head start when it comes to being a Jewish mother. For one, you know the proper attitudes toward treating your dying husband. He should take the homemade pastry intended for the shiva? I think not. Besides, he'd mess up the platters. (Shiva is Judaism's weeklong period of grief and mourning for the seven first-degree relatives: father, mother, son, daughter, brother, sister, or spouse. It's covered in detail in a later chapter.)

Jewish mothers also know the appropriate attitudes toward guilt, cleanliness, and love. The last, of course, is the most important, and explains why Jewish mothers take such pride in their children. Think of these qualities as a reflex, like blinking when you get a cinder in your eye, coughing when you have a cold, or jumping up when you see a mouse. How can you tell if you have the Jewish mother reflex? Here are some hints.

* You don't drink, because it would interfere with your suffering.
* In anticipation of the cleaning crew coming, you clean the entire house. The cleaners arrive and scrub all day. When they leave, you clean the house. Hey: There's clean and then there's Jewish mother *clean*.
* You greet people with hugs and kisses, even if you're meeting them for the first time.

But even those born with the Jewish mother reflex can benefit from having their skills sharpened. That's the purpose of this chapter. Consider it boot camp for Jewish mamas. You'll get trained in the other qualities of the Jewish mother—excessive worry, education, food, and advocacy—later on.

Guilt Trip

Q: *How many Jewish mothers does it take to change a light bulb?*

A: *From the Jewish mother: (Sigh) "Don't bother; I'll sit in the dark. I don't want to be a nuisance to anyone."*

Jewish Mother Kissing

Jewish mothers give real kisses. Follow these steps:

1. Approach and grab the person's face with your right hand, cupping their chin in your palm and digging your fingers into their cheeks. Squeeze hard enough to leave marks and yell, "Such a punim [POO-nim]!", which means "Such a face!"
2. Kiss the person hard on the cheek, making the kissing noise. Be sure to leave a big red lipstick stain.
3. Release the face.
4. Note: If you're elderly, you can also add a few cheek pinches.

A friend who wishes to remain unnamed sent this comment: My mother is a typical Jewish mother. Once she was on jury duty. They sent her home. She insisted SHE was guilty.

Ach, you call it "guilt." We call it "concern" and "caring." I asked my friend Judith Pasko what she thought of when I say "Jewish mother." She replied: "IT'S NEVER ENOUGH." Clearly, she has passed level one.

Guilt 101 (No Prerequisites)

All mothers do guilt. All mothers do food. But Jewish mothers have 3,000 years of constant practice at making you feel guilty for not consuming a gallon of Cherry Garcia on top of a side of beef and a loaf of marble rye. While wearing your raincoat in case it should storm suddenly.

Imagine these scenarios. They are 100 percent fictional . . .

Jewish mother to son, age five:
"You call that a dinner? A broiled chicken, a veal cutlet, two rib steaks, a pair of lamb chops, and a loaf of bread is just a nosh. At least have some mushroom barley soup. It will stick to your ribs. You're so skinny. A skeleton. People will think I never gave you a decent meal in your life. And stand up straight. You slouch like my grandfather."

Jewish mother to son, age fifteen:

"Don't forget your umbrella. I should worry? I know you're a capable boy, a real mensch. You got your galoshes? A hat? Your raincoat? So what if you're with your bubbie [grandmother] in Boca? She's been known to forget an umbrella. She's no spring chicken, you know."

Marriage

In the United States, the average age of marriage is 26 years for men, 25 years for women. It's higher on average in the world: 28.7 years for men, 26.8 years for women. In case you're wondering (and I know you are), Britney Spears and Jason Alexander have the record for the shortest marriage: 55 hours. Those wild kids. Jewish children marry at an older age, as you'll read later.

Jewish mother to son, age twenty:

"So you've decided to major in economics and computer science. Whatever this is, I'm sure it's fine but I don't know from it. Of course, pride of my life, you can do whatever makes you happy. But your father and I have decided that you'll be happiest if you become a doctor, lawyer, or accountant. Worst case, a dentist . . . as long as it's an orthodontist."

Jewish mother to son, age twenty-two:

"We are so delighted that you enrolled in medical school and moved from your home to your own apartment. So what if you chose to move so far away—twenty miles and a bridge we have to pass. Your father and I will be over tomorrow to bring some food. You don't know where to buy any food in a strange city and you're probably starving. I'll clean your kitchen shelves, line them with Contact paper, and stock the cans of tuna. I bought some plastic slipcovers for your futon (in my day, we had sofas, but what do I know?) and your lamps. I got you some paper plates and a sweater too."

Do Not Be Fooled! Accept Only the Real Jewish Mother!

"The Jewish Mother" was a restaurant in Williamsburg, Virginia, that was very popular with the William and Mary students, just a few minutes' drive off campus. It was known for the combination of great sandwiches (think New York deli) and great nightlife, since the place hosted local bands on the weekends. The original "Jewish Mother," located in Virginia Beach, was supposedly named after one of the owner's actual Jewish Mothers, who influenced the menu. Sadly, the Williamsburg Jewish Mother burned down sometime in 1999, and was never rebuilt. (Thank you to Jessica Swantek Conklin, a wonderful young lady.)

The Portable Jewish Mother

Jewish mother to son, age twenty-five:

"Did you hear that Mrs. Schwartz's son Jason is already married and he's a year younger than you? Your father and I are wondering when you'll get married. I know all this medical school stuff keeps you very busy. (Aside to husband: He's ripping out my heart and chewing on it. For this we got him laser eye surgery? For this we had his teeth straightened? And we paid good money for that fancy-schmancy college? Is it so terrible to want to have your son married before you've got one foot in the grave?)

Response from son (who didn't go to medical school but who did get a degree in economics from Princeton and now works as an analyst on Wall Street):

Sometimes, when I'm having dinner, I forget to clean my plate even though children are starving in China. Sometimes I don't bring five sandwiches and a slice of cake when I go out just because I might get hungry later. We have food stores in Jersey. Mom— Mom, really, I swear—we don't need you to buy us tuna fish, we can buy it ourselves . . . it was on sale. I see. So you bought ten cans. If we take the tuna, will you at least let us leave the saltines and rye bread?

No, really, I can't possibly eat any more cake, I'm still full from dinner—all right we'll take a slice. In case we get hungry on the train. No, Mom, that's not a slice, that's a quarter of a cake . . . yes, it's my favorite, I know you made it just for me, I do appreciate

that you slaved all day over a hot stove, no, don't be upset, I'll take the damn cake. . . .

Sometimes I almost go out in the rain without my umbrella and risk catching my death of cold.

Thank you to my son Charles, a truly exemplary son. And while you're reading this, be sure to put in your briefcase the small folded raincoat I bought you from the Dollar Store. And remind me: I got you and Rebecca some nice fresh tomatoes from the farm stand. Your father and I will bring them over this weekend.

Advanced Guilt (Prerequisite Guilt 101)
Have you heard this one?

A Jewish man calls his mother in Florida. "Mom, how are you?"

"Not too good," says the mother. "I've been very weak."

The son says, "Why are you so weak?"

She says, "Because, I haven't eaten in thirty-eight days."

"Mama," the man says, "that's terrible. Why haven't you eaten in thirty-eight days?"

The mother answers, "Because I didn't want my mouth to be filled with food if you should call."

The Portable Jewish Mother

Nice, eh? This story works in both guilt and food, clearly showing that this Jewish mother has attained Master status. Jewish children, let this be a lesson to you. Once the Jewish mother has mastered guilt, you're powerless. Nothing you do will ever be right again. Smile, nod, and accept your fate. Here's another example of master guiltmongers at work:

Four Jewish brothers have become successful doctors and lawyers. One night, they chat after having dinner together, discussing the birthday gifts they've given to their elderly mother, who lived far away in another city. The first says, "I had a big house built for Mama."

The second says, "I had a hundred-thousand-dollar theater built in the house."

The third says, "I had my Mercedes dealer deliver her an SL600 with chauffeur."

The fourth says, "Listen to this. You know how Mama loves reading the Torah. And you know, too, she can't read anymore because she can't see very well. I met this rabbi who told me about a parrot that can recite the entire Torah. It took twenty rabbis twelve years to teach him. I had to pledge to contribute $100,000 a year for twenty years to the temple. Let me tell you . . . it was worth it. All Mama has to do is name a chapter and verse and the parrot will recite it." The other brothers are impressed.

After her birthday when all the gifts have been received, Mom sends out her thank-you notes.

To her first son, she writes: "Milton, the house you built is huge. I live in only one room, but I have to clean the whole house. Thanks anyway."

To her second son, she writes: "Marvin, I am too old to travel. I stay home, I have my groceries delivered, so I never use the Mercedes . . . and the driver you hired is a Nazi. The thought was good. Thanks."

The Torah

Torah refers to the first books of the Hebrew Bible: Genesis, Exodus, Leviticus, Numbers, and Deuteronomy. The Torah is also known as the Five Books of Moses or the Pentateuch. The term can also refer to Judaism's written and oral law.

To her third son, she writes: "Menachim, you gave me an expensive theater with Dolby sound, it could hold fifty people, but all my friends are dead, I've lost my hearing, and I'm nearly blind. I'll never use it. Thank you for the gesture just the same."

To her fourth son, she writes: "Dearest Melvin, you were the only son to have the good sense to give a little thought to your gift. The chicken was delicious. Thank you."

Guilt Gone Astray

Here's a serious view of guilt gone astray from a friend of mine, whom I'll leave anonymous. It's serious, but shows that excessive guilt can cause scars:

At my home, we had the guilt. My mother was entirely supportive of what we wanted to do, be it extracurricular activities in high school or a major in college. Of course, that support came with the hurt tone and opinion that she supports it but wouldn't I be happier if . . . ?

I always seemed to be disappointing my mother. She took many of my choices as personal attacks. I deliberately had an African-American roommate and Asian girlfriend just to drive my mother nuts, if you ask her. Mom clearly expected me to have a nice Jewish girlfriend despite the fact that religion was not a part of my lifestyle. The family never went to shul, and I was told I had to go through with my bar mitzvah so I could receive gifts from the family to help me finance college (in the end, I tapped the money to help buy a car and an engagement ring for the nice not-Jewish girl I married). Religion was an obligation, not a lifestyle and I never saw my mother act as if it mattered until I announced I was marrying outside the faith. Then it became a big deal.

Twenty-six years and two grandchildren later, my mother still doesn't attend services so I'm left to scratch my head.

The following friend was even more scathing in his portrait of the Jewish mother gone to extremes. In this instance, the gorgon was his mother-in-law. She's the worst example I've yet found—and I hope that she remains the model of the Jewish Mother Gone Astray:

In this book, we have affectionate portraits of Jewish women born at the end of the nineteenth century, who denied themselves food so the children would never be hungry. Love and brisket shared the plate.

We also have the newer version—sexy, tan, toned Glam-Ma, bedecked in bling, hiding a naughty tattoo, thinking about a Harley or the young cashier.

But there are transitional figures, such as my former mother-in-law, now in her seventies. A traditionalist, she reads Jewish papers and defends Israel; says Yiskor for her parents; keeps a kosher home. Married for more than fifty years; she has children and grandchildren. Her house is neat; her hair is coiffed; she is trim; her dress is timelessly modest. Simultaneously a modern woman, she worked when her children were in school. She reads current fiction and upscale cooking magazines; she plays tennis; she e-mails, she shops for bargains but never overspends; she would never have cosmetic surgery. She is efficient; she balances the checkbook and makes the investments. Her determined thrift made possible a beautiful home and a lovely retirement house in Florida.

But only *superficially* does she embody anything meaningful from either world. Perhaps because she was a poor urban child and saw her parents—gentle, unsophisticated people born in the shtetl—dominated by economic forces they didn't understand and couldn't master, she decided to take control. And did she ever!

That might seem a commendable study in feminine empowerment, but love demands a certain untidiness of spirit, and her soul is swept clean of emotional clutter. Her kitchen shines, but what price such glory? She insisted on having everything right; she pushed everyone around her to attain perfection. Her husband, quiet and diligent, long ago became a buck private in her army, arranging the placemats on the table. Her children, wounded and alienated, fled—one to the other end of the continent, the other into mental illness. She smiles and calls people "Dear," or "darling," but her manner is politely, fatally critical. While appearing to make a helpful suggestion or offering advice, she implies that only she knows how something should be done. Her victims shrink and shrink; when the meal ends, they are vacuumed up with the crumbs.

She will be eulogized as a model mother, wife, grandmother; a good, upstanding Jew, but only those who have lived at close range will know the effects. Ironically, her chicken soup and mandel bread are so purged of unhealthy fat, salt, and sugar that they are parody food—the culinary equivalent of her empty spirit.

"And I alone have escaped to tell thee."

—Ishmael

Here's my advice for Jewish-mothers-in-training: Use guilt gently and sparingly, as you would jalapeño peppers. A little goes a very long way. When in doubt, hold back on the blame and give the kids the benefit of the doubt. After all, you can always guilt them to death later.

Cleanliness

> *Neurotics build castles in the sky.*
> *Psychotics live in them.*
> *Jewish mothers clean them.*

—Rita Rudner and others

My friend Gary Goldstein proves this with a story about his Jewish mother: "When I was a kid, I was playing with a dirty tennis ball in my room. I bounced it too hard and it hit the ceiling, leaving a black smudge. When my mom saw it she screamed, 'I was on my hands and knees all day yesterday cleaning that ceiling!' I rest my case."

Traditional Jewish mothers are obsessively clean. Jeri Cipriano, daughter of Claire Schlefar, said: "My mom also went beyond the 'wear clean underwear—you never know.' When I was a little girl she actually polished the soles of my saddle shoes as well."

This Jewish mother haiku expresses it well:

After the warm rain
The sweet smell of camellias.
Did you wipe your feet?

I came home from a vacation a bit early once to find my children cleaning the house. My daughter was wiping down the cabinets with a bleach solution; my son was washing the floor on his hands and knees. Naturally, the entire house had been tidied, vacuumed, and dusted. Tragically, the kids hadn't even had a party. They wouldn't want the mess.

Quick Quiz

Directions: How does a Jewish husband make his wife scream for six hours during sex? Write your answer below:

_____

_____

_____

_____

Answer

Three men are discussing their previous night's lovemaking. The Italian says, "My wife, I rubbed her all over with fine olive oil, then we make wonderful love. She screamed for five minutes."

The Frenchman says, "I smooth sweet butter on my wife's body, then we made passionate love. She screamed for half an hour."

The Jew says, "I covered my wife's body with schmaltz. We made love and she screamed for six hours."

The others say, "Six hours? How did you make her scream for six hours?"

He shrugs. "I wiped my hands on the drapes."

- -

Schmaltz

Schmaltz is chicken or goose fat that has been rendered. You can then cook with it or eat it as a spread, like butter. Since schmaltz is kosher, it's commonplace in the homes of European Jews, who couldn't use butter or lard in preparing meats. My friend Stephan Gary Kravitz loves onions fried in schmaltz, but we don't let him eat them because they're both fattening and bad for his arteries. Today, we often use the word *schmaltz* to describe something that is overly sentimental, such as a play or song.

- -

Here's my advice for Jewish-Mothers-in-training: Keep the house tidy but not eat-off-the floor clean. After all, if the kids are eating off the floor, you got bigger problems on your hands.

CHAPTER 8

The Importance of Education

No jokes here: A true Jewish mother will sacrifice all so her children get an education. Even if it means dealing with that teacher who's a schmuck (you know the one I mean).

Your child earns an M.D. degree. Repeat after me, Jewish mothers: "What? No Ph.D., too?" (This works equally well with any level of education.) Jews have always had relative success in whichever society they lived. One good reason: Jews valued literacy and education before many other societies did. Jokes aside, why the Jewish emphasis on education? Why do Jewish mothers stress education to their children? There are many theories; below are my favorites.

Theory #1: Tikkun Olam

Tikkun olam is a Hebrew phrase that translates to "repairing the world." It's important in Judaism and is often used to explain the Jewish concept of social justice. In some explanations, the more *mitzvot* that are performed, the closer the world will be toward perfection.

Some observant Jews believe that acts of tikkun olam will either trigger or fulfill the prophesied coming of the messiah. Nonetheless, acts of tikkun olam are performed not because they are the law but because they make the world a better place. In progressive streams of Judaism—Conservative, Reform, and Reconstructionist strands—tikkun olam has taken on political and religious significance in that it implies that Jews should work toward social justice. Education is one of the best ways to achieve this. Hence, the emphasis on formal learning.

Mitzvot

Mitzvot, a Hebrew word for "commandment," refers to the 613 commandments in the Torah or any Jewish law at all. The term *mitzvah* has also come to express any act of human kindness, such as the burial of the body of an unknown person. According to the teachings of Judaism, all moral laws are, or are derived from, divine commandments.

Theory #2: Sink or Swim

For immigrant Jews, the drive to secure financial well-being within an individualistic society meant that, for the majority, educational priorities were not open to discussion. School came first. Education was the key to survival and success. As a result, most American Jews enrolled their children in public schools, relegating Jewish education to weekday afternoons or weekend mornings. Jewish mothers supported their children's educational progress, driving them to succeed.

As the children of successive waves of immigrants passed through the public school system and climbed the country's socioeconomic ladder, the Jewish attachment to public education grew into a true love affair. Many Jews believed that the schools were responsible not only for the rapid Americanization and success of Jews themselves but also for the relatively low levels of intolerance and bigotry in American society at large—when compared to the pogroms and institutionalized anti-Semitism in many European countries. As one Jewish leader put it, "The schools were a place where the children of the high and low, rich and poor, Protestant, Catholics, and Jews mingle together, play together, and are taught that we are a free people, striving to elevate mankind and to respect one another." Jewish mothers recognized this early on.

Theory #3: No Other Choices

In Europe, Jews were often forbidden by law to own land or work the land. How could they make a living in traditional farming communities? Jews were left with crafts, trade, and professions—careers that required significant education. Craftspeople and traders had to know mathematics; doctors had to know medicine; attorneys had to know the law. Traders mastered languages.

Theory #4: Taking the Long View

Philosopher Jeremy Bentham argued that obligatory acts are those that bestow the greatest pleasure on the greatest number. A true Jewish mother would reply, "Pleasure, schmleasure. You want pleasure; I'll give you pleasure; I'll let you live another day. Now go do your homework."

Jewish mothers are indeed interested in their children's happiness, but they take the long view: Children should have happiness throughout their entire lives, not mere short-term pleasure. Jewish mothers invented delayed gratification. Thus, a Jewish mother would say:

* "You do your school work now and you watch television later if there is time; your school work is more important; you need to learn all you can so you can make something of yourself."
* "I know you would rather stay up and watch television, but you will be tired in the morning and you won't want to get up and you won't be able to pay attention in school; so turn off the television and go to bed."

Add in the guilt and you've got it: Another five minutes of TV tonight, and you'll end up on welfare as an adult rather than being a proctologist running your own practice.

For Example . . .
My dear friend Emily Bengels, the brilliant and accomplished daughter of university professor and Jewish mother par excellence Barbara Bengels, contributed this assessment of her mother's attitudes toward education:

I'm trying to think what is notably Jewish about my relationship with my mother. Of course there were the shared experiences we had with blending latkes and devouring Sunday morning matzoh brei or blintzes . . . and then there have been hours of my trying to tap her memory for anything that might help me with genealogical research . . . or our attending lots of shows with Jewish themes (Rags, Ragtime, The Rothschilds, Fiddler . . .) but I think those are more token recipes, place names and performances than what really made my Mom's loving ways Jewish.

Shavuot

Shavuot is a Jewish holiday that falls on the sixth day of the Hebrew month of Sivan (corresponding to late May or early June). One of the three Biblical pilgrimage festivals mandated by the Torah, it marks the day the Torah was given at Mount Sinai. Observant Jewish mothers celebrate this holiday with their families.

The essential "Jewish mother" element about Mom is her eagerness to advocate our education, and encourage us to do the same. From writing newspaper articles about how she enjoyed chauffeuring us to and from lessons to being a recognized advocate of good teaching within our school district, Mom always lets us

know that we are important and our education is important. I never knew Mom to be concerned about our grades; rather, our learning and caring about what we were learning is foremost on her mind. She models the love of learning in her own constant state of being in the midst of reading several books!

A Taste of Honey

In the Jewish tradition, learning is a sweet thing—and I'm not exaggerating. A medieval tradition links honey to reading and the festival of Shavuot. It's generally accepted that Shavuot is the anniversary of the Jewish people receiving the Torah after Moses descended from Mount Sinai. During the Middle Ages, young children were first brought to the classroom to begin their education on Shavuot. The letters of the Hebrew alphabet were covered with honey or candy, fulfilling the Hebrew verse, "How pleasing is Your word to my palate, sweeter than honey." The teacher would read each letter, and the children would repeat after him. Each child licked the honey from the letter as he learned it. Naturally, children would link learning to sweets.

This Jewish mother haiku expresses it well:

Beyond Valium
The peace of knowing one's child
Is an internist.

The Results of the Jewish Belief in Education and Hard Work

Most of the Nobel laureates have been men—and they continue to be—but a few Jewish women have managed to break into this elite club. One of the most impressive is Jewish mother Rosalyn Yalow, who received the Albert Lasker Award for Basic Medical Research in 1976 and the Nobel Prize in 1977. Her hard work and determination are inspiring.

Rosalyn Sussman Yalow

Yalow, born in 1921, is a medical physicist and the co-winner of the 1977 Nobel Prize in medicine for her development of the radioimmunoassay (RIA) technique. Born Rosalyn Sussman in New York City, she was educated at Hunter College. Yalow wanted to pursue a graduate degree in physics, but realized that it was unlikely that any worthwhile graduate school would admit and fund a woman. She also knew that given the prevailing anti-Semitism of the day, a *Jewish* woman stood even less chance of earning a graduate degree. So she decided to take a position as a secretary, a common occupation for women back then. However, right before she began taking dictation and making coffee, the fates intervened: The University of Illinois offered her an assistantship in physics. Why did they choose a woman? All the men were off fighting in World War II.

Yalow was the only woman among the department's 400 members. In 1943, Yalow married her husband Aaron. She completed her Ph.D. two years later. Then Yalow took a job with the Bronx Veterans Administration Hospital setting up their radio-isotope service. Collaborating with Solomon Bernson, she developed a radioisotope tracing technique called RIA to measure minute quantities of different substances in the bloodstream. To date, RIA has been used to measure an astonishingly wide variety of substances, including hormones, vitamins, and enzymes. Yalow and Bernson did not patent RIA, selflessly donating their accomplishments to science rather than lining their own pockets.

Yitzhak Rabin

Israeli Prime Minister Yitzhak Rabin (1922–1995) was awarded the 1994 Nobel Peace Prize, along with Yasser Arafat and Shimon Peres, for his role in the creation of the Oslo Accords. His mother was proud.

Thanks to her children, Benjamin and Elanna, Rosalyn Yalow qualifies as a Jewish mother! (And both her children have done very well, since you asked.)

Test Yourself

Directions: Circle *true* or *false* for each statement.

1 Jewish scientist Paul Ehrlich won a Nobel Prize for discovering a treatment for syphilis.

    True   False

2 Jewish scientist and Jewish mother Rita Levi-Montalcini won the Nobel Prize for her work on nerve growth factor (with Stanley Cohen).

    True   False

3 Jewish physician and scientist Bernard Katz won the Nobel Prize in medicine for his work in neuromuscular transmission.

    True   False

4 Jewish physicist Murray Gell-Mann won the Nobel Prize in physics 1969 for introducing the concept of "quarks."

    True   False

5 Jewish humanitarian, writer, and Holocaust survivor Elie Wiesel won the Nobel Peace Prize.

    True   False

6 Jewish author Saul Bellow won the Nobel Prize for literature.

    True   False

The Portable Jewish Mother

7 Jewish physician and scientist Howard Temin won the 1975 Nobel Prize in medicine.

     True   False

8 Jewish physicist David Lee won the Nobel Prize in physics for his work on superfluidity.

     True   False

9 Jewish physician and scientist Joshua Lederberg won the Nobel Prize in medicine for his discovery of viral transduction.

     True   False

10 Jewish economist Paul Samuelson won a Nobel Prize in economics.

     True   False

11 Jewish author and Jewish mother Nadine Gordimer, a native of South Africa, won the Nobel Prize in literature.

     True   False

12 Jewish chemist Aaron Klug won the Nobel Prize in chemistry for his work on x-ray analysis of biomolecules.

     True   False

13 Jewish writer Isaac Bashevis Singer won the 1978 Nobel Prize in literature.

     True   False

14 Jewish economist Milton Friedman won a Nobel Prize in economics.

     True   False

15 Prime Minister of Israel Yitzhak Rabin won a Nobel Peace Prize.

     True   False

How many of the following fashion designers are Jewish?

∗ Calvin Klein
∗ Ralph Lauren
∗ Pauline Trigere
∗ Isaac Mizrahi
∗ Kenneth Cole

· ·

Ralph Lauren

Born Ralph Lifschitz to Jewish immigrants in 1939, Lauren has risen to great prominence as a fashion designer. Ralph was sixteen years old when he changed his last name from "Lifschitz" to "Lauren." Brother Jerry followed suit. Were Ralph and Jerry trying to cover their Jewish roots? Both men argue that given the rampant anti-Semitism of the times, they were just being savvy businessmen. I must agree.

· ·

Answers

You're too smart to be fooled: Every one of the fifteen Jewish achievers listed won a Nobel Prize. It's no stretch to conclude that Jews have made and continue to make major contributions to the cultural, scientific, political, and economic life of the United States. For example, 37 percent of all United States Nobel Prize winners in the twentieth century were Jewish. Who do you think supervised their education, eh? Their patient, loving, and farsighted Jewish mothers. And, as you read, some of those Jewish mothers even won Nobels of their own.

And all the fashion designers are Jewish. This education thing pays off big time.

In the next chapter, we'll explore the importance of love and unconditional support—and how a Jewish mother is an expert on both.

$\mathscr{Love} = \mathscr{Food}$

See? The thirty-six hours in labor
was all worth it.

After guilt, guilt, and more guilt, Jewish mothers are characterized by love for their children. Some call it excessive love, but to those of us who identify as Jewish mothers, you can never show too much love.

There's a wonderful Yiddish word for the pleasure we take in our children: *naches* (pronounced NOKH-ess). Jewish mothers use the word *naches* to describe the special love that you can only get from your offspring's success. You use the word like this: "Ah, I get such naches from my son David now that he has [choose one]: won the Pulitzer Prize in literature / been elected the first Jewish president of the United States / cured cancer / finally learned to tie his own shoelaces."

For a Jewish mother, unconditional love is inextricably tied to excessive food. And not just any food, either: only the best, traditional food. Remember: Any time a person goes into a delicatessen and orders pastrami on white bread, somewhere a Jewish mother groans in disgust.

You'll learn how to master Jewish mother love in this chapter. You'll learn that it's inextricably tied to food. So have a snack (a little nosh) and settle in to read.

Unconditional Love and Support

More than anything else, Jewish mothers give their children love. My dear friend Lenore Strober had refined this to an art form:

She had enough love for her husband, her five wonderful children—Brad, Andy, Allison, Rod, Shari—all her friends, and all her students at Commack High School South. Tragically, she left this world much too soon. I wrote this eulogy for her.

Tribute to a Jewish Mother
Dear Jerry, Brad, Andy, Allison, Rod, Shari,

Lenore touched so many lives that I know you are going to get many letters like this, letters that describe her generosity, kindness, and love. People will write about the wonderful parties and outrageous desserts (the cheesecakes, chocolate cakes, seven-layer cookies). Perhaps they'll remember meeting her in Pathmark, as she pushed two carts piled high with food and several kids in tow, preparing for those parties and caring for her family. Everyone remembers that her house and heart were always open for us all. How could we not? It was so for more than a quarter of a century and helped shape our lives.

People from Commack High School South will describe the mounds of papers she graded every night so her students could learn

to write. They'll talk about Lenore at the annual English Regents "Body Shop," wheedling a few extra points for a miscreant whom she had nurtured, as she softly said, "We can pass this paper. Look how nicely he made his periods. They're all right-side up." When we finished laughing, the kid would magically have passed the Regents. Nothing would have been served by keeping him—and his buddies—behind, and Lenore knew it. Scores of kids owe their high school graduations to her.

Some of us remember holding up signs with "dirty words" outside her classroom window at South, trying to get her to curse. We never had any success at all, but we sure made her blush.

We all remember asking, "Lenore, got any pictures of the kids?" and she'd flip out a few hundred, complete with extensive narration. We kvelled to the kids' latest accomplishments, and danced at all the bar/bas mitzvahs and weddings. We enjoyed hearing about the grandkids, too, and everyone's professional triumphs. We knew when Brad and his brood came for a visit, when Andy bought a big house, when Allison had the twins, when Shari subbed, when Rod got his puppies. We loved it all.

I can write about all that, but I'd like to explain what Lenore meant to me: unconditional love. She gave us love with no strings attached, love from her endless supply, like a magical well that never ran dry. How one little lady with so much richness at home had so much to share remains one of life's mysteries, but her well of goodness never ran dry. I came to her first when I passed my Ph.D. orals, making a special trip from Stony Brook. She bought me a beautiful gold heart when I left South in 1984—what could be a better symbol of Lenore than a heart?

There will never be another like her.

Roots and Wings

There are two lasting things that Jewish mothers give our children: roots and wings. There's some truth to this cliché: roots help kids feel secure and grounded; wings allow them to become independent adults. Okay, so maybe Jewish mothers are a little heavy on the roots and a little light on the wings, but we give it our best shot.

For instance, my friend Jewish mother Margie Glazer wrote this poem when her daughter Dara left for college. What greater love is there than helping your child grow up and become independent? Margie is a great example of a Jewish mother who gave her daughter both roots and wings.

To Dara

*Sets limits for her daughter
and feels guilty for the crying.
She doesn't know it is
simply the noise of growing.*

*Tries to prepare her child
for going away to college
when she's still in kindergarten.*

*Wants to send her child
off with a booklet
for surviving tornadoes
in New York City.*

*Leaves her child
at college, notices
the Do Not Call sign*

*but fears her child
will feel unloved
if she doesn't call.*

*Dreams she is in THE city
looking but not finding
the train that will bring her
to her daughter.*

*On the side of the tracks,
buildings and trees are missing.
There are holes in the sandy dirt,
and footprints run off like water.*

*There is still no train, and
there's been no bombing,
just an uprooting.*

—Margie Glazer

127

I'm Guilty as Charged

Since I'm shameless, I asked my daughter Sammi how I shape up as a Jewish mother. After all, I'm supposed to be the expert! I'll pass along her assessment.

There are many different stereotypes that go along with a Jewish mother. My mother fits them all—from excessive pride to worrying about me. She tells me that she misses me when I go to college twenty minutes from home. A great example is from yesterday when I called home and said that I wasn't feeling well. I told her that I thought it might be my allergies, so she shows up at school with daytime cold pills, nighttime cold sleeping liquid, a box of tissues, the newspapers, and a big container of chicken noodle soup that I was told to "drink right away. And as hot as you can take it."

As much as I say that my mother is very stereotypical, she is a wonderful mother. It's great to know that someone is worrying about me and wants to know how my day went. She carries around pictures of me at every event that I have ever attended and shows them to every person that she meets. It's even starting to rub off on my father! When I won "Junior Woman of the Year," he sent out a mass e-mail to every one of his friends telling them how proud he and my mother were.

Fortunately or unfortunately—depending on the size of your tuchus (rear end)—Jewish mothers often provide unconditional love via unending food.

You Don't Like My Food?

Did you hear the one about the bum who walked up to the Jewish mother on the street and said, "Lady, I haven't eaten in three days."

She replied: "Force yourself."

My paternal grandmother, Paula Neu, was a heroic Jewish mama disguised as a tiny and sweet blue-haired old lady. She engineered her family's escape from Nazi Germany. She brought her husband and two children with her, as well as her mother. (Her father had died.) My grandmother always worked outside the home, side-by-side with my grandfather, to establish a life in America. Her mother lived with them and kept house. Since my great-grandmother lived a remarkably long and productive life, my grandmother never had to cook. She figured, Why learn?

After her mother died, my grandmother finally had to learn to cook. By then, she decided that it was hardly worth the effort, so she mastered only two foods: Hebrew National hot dogs and one cake. The cake was versatile, however. Over the basic slab of yeast dough, she sprinkled crumbs for her delicious crumb cake. She made a sour cherry version, an apple version, and a plum version. Since I wasn't the quickest kid on the block, it took me years to figure out that she could only make one cake.

When my husband and I got married, he and my grandmother hit it off right away. The first time we came to visit, she made him the crumb cake, the sour cherry version, the apple version, and the plum version. We're talking a table groaning with cake. When he couldn't consume four monstrously large yeast cakes at one sitting, she stared up at him and said, "So, nu? You don't like mine cakes?" Clearly, she had mastered the art of combining food and guilt.

For those of you just starting out, here's the equation:

The Importance of Food

food = love
more food = more love
most food = most love

The Portable Jewish Mother

Alas! My grandmother's recipe is lost because she never wrote it down. I used to watch her bake The Cake, but she didn't measure most ingredients. When I implored her to measure, she used a metric scale rather than measuring cups. All this math was beyond me so I went to my traditional German-Jewish cookbooks. Following is a recipe for a cake like the one my grandmother made. The cake is not overly sweet or cakey; rather, it's similar to a thick slice of bread with crumbs.

In place of crumbs, you can arrange sliced Italian prune plums or baking apples in rows like obedient school children. Then bake. Do not use prepared pie filling in place of fresh fruit. Fey! The cake is especially nice topped with gently whipped heavy cream with just a bit of sugar in it.

Ingredients for Cake

1	(¼-oz) package active dry yeast (2½ teaspoons)
1	cup warm milk
½	cup plus 1 tablespoon sugar
1	tablespoon fresh lemon juice
3¾	cups plus 2 tablespoons all-purpose flour
1½	teaspoons salt
2	large eggs, at room temperature for 30 minutes
1½	teaspoons vanilla
1½	sticks (¾ cup) unsalted butter, room temperature

Ingredients for Crumbs

¾	cup sugar
1½	cups all-purpose flour
1	teaspoon cinnamon
1½	sticks (¾ cup) butter at room temperature
1	teaspoon vanilla

To Make the Cake: (The dough is hard to mix by hand, so use a food processor or a sturdy stand mixer.)

1. In a large bowl or the bowl of the food processor, mix yeast, ¼ cup warm milk, and 1 tablespoon sugar.
2. Let sit until foamy, about 5 minutes. (If it doesn't foam, the yeast is dead. Give the yeast a decent burial and start over with a new package of yeast.)
3. Mix lemon juice and remaining ¾ cup milk. It will curdle.
4. Add 3¾ cups flour, salt, eggs, vanilla, and remaining ½ cup sugar to yeast mixture.
5. Add curdled milk and mix to make dough.
6. Add butter, a spoon at a time, until dough is silky and elastic. This will take 5 to 8 minutes. The dough will be sticky.
7. Sprinkle with remaining 2 tablespoons flour, cover bowl with a clean towel, and let rise until doubled in bulk, 1½ to 2 hours.

To Make the Crumbs:
1. Mix all ingredients to form crumbs. Chill

To Finish:
1. Butter a 13" × 9" pan.
2. Spread cake dough in pan. Sprinkle on half of crumbs.
3. Let cake rise until almost doubled in bulk, 1 to 1½ hours.
4. Add rest of crumbs and bake at 350° about 45–60 minutes. The crumbs should be golden brown.

How to Feed Like a Jewish Mother
Feed early, often, and constantly. Do not be constrained by the child's age: A child of any age can easily fit on your lap. Ten, twenty, thirty, forty, fifty years old is fine—after all, they'll always be your children even if they do need a shave.

Three Close Friends Weigh In on the Issue of Food
Michelle Stern is a rabbinical student at the Reconstructionist Rabbinical College. I met her when she dated my son while they were in high school. When each found a different beloved, I decided to keep Michelle for myself because I adore her. After all, she loves my cooking, especially my brownies.

Michelle has worked as a Jewish educator to people of all ages. She has also worked as a service and community leader and a chaplain. She will, with God's help, be ordained in 2010. She wrote this for me:

I recently visited my boyfriend's parent's home for the first time, though I have met them before. Upon arrival, I was jet lagged, tired and hungry after a long day of travels across the country. His mother, a Jewish woman in her late fifties from Mexico City, asked me if I would like an omelet. I said that would be fine. Ten minutes later, I sat down to a plate of scrambled eggs, a whole sliced tomato, and toast. In addition, white fish and Israeli pickles were taken out of the fridge. Orange juice and water were poured. For an afternoon post-flight snack, this was a feast! I was completely nourished—not just by the food, but by the company and the hospitality.

In the Bible, Abraham and Sarah welcomed strangers into their tent, fed them, washed their feet, and offered places of rest. For Jews, a kitchen can be the center of a home and the central place where someone can come to feel welcomed. In feeding others, I believe, Jews themselves are enriched and nourished. Nourishment and nurturing seem to be one in Jewish culture. Between the meal from my boyfriend's mother and the hug I received from his father as he whispered in his Israeli accent "Welcome Home," I knew I was.

Jillian Dorans is my daughter Sammi's best friend. They've been buddies since they were five years old and we all adore the wonderful Jillian. Here's what she wrote about Jewish mothers and food:

> *I didn't think it was possible for a mother to try to feed you more (or love you more) than an Italian, but enter Laurie Rozakis, the Jewish mother par excellence. And although I am a Catholic, Mama Rozakis has inspired me to date a Jewish boy. Who wouldn't want to date a well-fed man taught to take orders from a woman?*

Chaya Goldish is a dear friend, a successful businesswoman, a fabulous Jewish mother, and the wife of the brilliant writer Meish Goldish. Her story describes how her family relates to food. It was the most unusual and emotional story I received.

> *My grandmother, Rochel Leah, survived World War II together with five of her six daughters (my mother is the middle child) ranging in age from seventeen to seven years old. Her husband, my grandfather, was taken to a "work camp" and did not survive. When I asked her how she had survived, she told me that it just never occurred to her that she wouldn't survive!*
>
> *After the war, the survivors were given food by the UNRA and other relief agencies. My grandmother said that she took small*

amounts of flour and sugar. She fried them in small amounts of oil, and this is what she fed her children for the first few days after they were liberated.

"Even though my heart ached to see the children crying with hunger and begging me to give them more food," she told me, "I did not give more than this." I don't know how my grandmother knew to do this, but it saved the lives of my mother and my aunts. After starving for more than a year, many survivors died during the first weeks of liberation from overeating.

I don't know if this is the reason my mother, contrary to the myth of Jewish mothers, told me that if I wasn't hungry, I shouldn't eat. Her motto when I was growing up was "Whether you eat the food or throw it into the garbage can, you can never use it again!"

CHAPTER 10

What, Me Worry?

Well, Yes.

You think the *Mad Magazine* mascot
Alfred E. Neuman invented that phrase? Pff.
It came from a Jewish mother. We invented worry
(and then lent a cup to the Catholics next door).

When people hear that you're writing a book about Jewish mothers, they're invariably supportive. And everyone has a story. It may not be their story, but rather the story from a friend or even the friend of a friend. The following story about worry came from the friend of a friend:

Mona mentioned that you are looking for stories by or about Jewish mothers. Mona and Peter told me that when they hear those two words "Jewish mother," they automatically think of me. . . . but in a good way.

I have a lot of stories to tell you. Here's my favorite: One day, my son had a friend over for a play date after school. Being a Jewish mother, I always preferred when kids played at my house so I could keep an eye on them. While the kids were snacking on some of my homemade brownies, I heard my son question his friend, "What are you so worried about? Whatever it is, well, you can tell my mother and she will worry for you. She is the Queen of Worriers."

—Judy Klau Pace

All Aboard the Worry Train

In previous chapters, you learned the basics of being a true Yiddishe mama: instilling guilt, cleaning like a maniac, and offering unconditional love and unending food. Now you're ready for prime time: worrying. It sounds like a lot to master, I know, but happily, it all fits together. The Worry Train looks like this:

* You worry because the child won't eat enough; you worry because they eat too much.
* You worry because your child may not have the GPA to get into medical school; you worry when they do get into medical school that they may not like their specialty.
* You worry that the house isn't clean enough and God forbid the kids will pick up something; you worry that the house is too clean and God forbid the kids won't build resistance to germs.

See? The Worry Train is a lovely, unified whole, which is why Jewish mothers have their very own stereotype.

You Can't Worry Too Much
A Jewish mother telegram: "Begin worrying. Details to follow." For the contemporary Jewish mother, just send the same message as an e-mail.

The following two Jewish mother haikus express the importance of worrying succinctly:

Sorry I'm not home
To take your call. At the tone
Please state your bad news.

Coroner's report—
"The deceased, wearing no hat,
caught his death of cold."

Someone once said: "There is no use worrying about things over which you have no control, and if you have control, you can do something about them instead of worrying." This person was clearly not describing Jewish mothers.

Worrywarts

How good are you at understanding the Jewish mother's psyche? Put a check mark next to each saying that you think applies to Jewish mothers.

○ 1. It is not work that kills, but worry. —*African Proverb*
○ 2. If something is wrong, fix it if you can, but train yourself not to worry. —*Mary Hemingway*
○ 3. Worry never fixes anything. —*Mary Hemingway*
○ 4. Do not anticipate trouble, or worry about what may never happen. Keep in the sunlight. —*Benjamin Franklin*

The Portable Jewish Mother

○ 5. If there be no remedy, why worry? —*Spanish Proverb*
○ 6. You're only here for a short visit. Don't hurry, don't worry. And be sure to smell the flowers along the way. —*Walter Hagen*

Answers

A Jewish mother wouldn't agree with a single one of these proverbs. Fey. They're all nonsense.

* Hard work never killed anyone. How do you think you get through law school?
* Worry can fix *anything*. It's better than Maalox.
* You keep in the sunlight as Franklin advises and you get a sunburn.
* You stop and smell the flowers as Walter Hagen advises, and you'll get stung by a bee. A big, nasty one, too.

The following chart shows what some "experts" say and how Jewish mothers interpret their words. And Mama is always right.

Smarty Pants

What They Say . . .	What a Jewish Mother Says . . .
I've seen many troubles in my time, only half of which ever came true. —*Mark Twain*	Yeah, but it's the other half that kill you.
As you leave, remember that 90 percent of what you worry about never happens. —*Catherine and Byron Pulsifer*	But it's that 10 percent that knocks you flat on your tuchus.
When I look back on all these worries, I remember the story of the old man who said on his deathbed that he had had a lot of trouble in his life, most of which had never happened. —*Winston Churchill*	Most, but not all. And the all is a killer.
Worrying about it takes precious time and attention away from your priorities and increases your feelings of dissatisfaction about life. —*Christina Winsey-Rudd*	What does she know? Like she's an expert?
Be too large for worry, too noble for anger. —*Christian D. Larson*	His name says it all.
Pack up your troubles in your old kit bag, and smile, smile, smile. —*George Asaf*	What is that man on?

If you see ten troubles coming down the road, you can be sure that nine will run into the ditch before they reach you. —*Calvin Coolidge*	That's one smart man. He knows the tenth is the doozy.
Worrying is like a rocking chair; it gives you something to do, but it doesn't get you anywhere. —*Anonymous*	Like hell it doesn't.
If you believe that feeling bad or worrying long enough will change a past or future event, then you are residing on another planet with a different reality system. —*William James*	We've already established that Jewish mothers have a different reality system.

Spreading the Wealth of Worry

Remember how I mentioned how everyone has a story about Jewish mothers to share? Well, they do. Here's what my dear friend Mary Ellen Snodgrass had to say. She's not a Jewish mother, but she's had experience with Jewish mothers other than me.

When I was in college at the University of North Carolina, I roomed next door to two Jewish students, Donna Reiss and Toni Oster. They complained about the surveillance of Jewish mothers during their freshman year, but nothing compared to my ubermother, a Baptist matriarch. Jews don't come close. When

I asked to invite Donna home for Thanksgiving, my mother was terrified she would screw up obligatory food traditions, like fish on Friday.

I was heartened to learn that Jewish mothers don't really have the market cornered on worry, even though it seems that way.

Don't Worry, Be Happy . . .

All mothers worry, but Jewish mothers worry a lot. Perhaps this is because they've had more than their fair share of worries in the past, as history reveals. You've already read all about anti-Semitism and the Jewish mother's very real fears. But Jewish mothers don't really need a reason to worry. We invent our own. Take this quiz to find out what real Jewish mothers obsess about.

Part 1: True/False
Directions: Circle *true* or *false* for each staement.

1 Jewish mothers in Kansas worry about tsunamis striking them from the South Pacific.
    True   False

2 Jewish mothers worry about consumers' easily shakable confidence.

  True   False

3 Jewish mothers in the Sahara Desert worry about their children drowning in deep water.

  True   False

4 Jewish mothers worry about the future of existentialism, the veracity of the unified field theory, and the rift between East Coast and West Coast rappers.

  True   False

5 Jewish mothers at the North Pole in the winter worry about their children sweating from the heat.

  True   False

6 Jewish mothers in Canada worry about Florida alligators coming out of the toilet and biting their kids on the tuchus. This will undo all their toilet training, of course.

  True   False

7 Jewish mothers worry about whether Nicole Richie and Paris Hilton will patch up their shaky friendship.

  True   False

8 Jewish mothers worry about the euro pounding the dollar.

  True   False

9 Jewish mothers worry about whether or not anyone will ever find Judge Crater.

  True   False

10 Jewish mothers worry about poor Bambi all alone in the woods. At night. In the dark.

True   False

Part 2: Essay

A hurricane blew across the Caribbean. It didn't take long for the expensive yacht to be swamped by high waves, sinking without a trace.

There were only two survivors: the boat's owner, a Jewish mother named Mildred, and its steward, Benny. Both managed to swim to the closest island. After reaching the deserted strip of land, the steward began crying, very upset that they would never be found. Mildred, however, was exceedingly calm, relaxing against a tree.

"Mildred, how can you be so calm?" cried Benny. "We're going to die on this lonely island. We'll never be discovered here. And besides, you're a Jewish mother. You *never* stop worrying."

"Sit down and listen to what I have to say, Benny," began the confident Mildred. "Five years ago I gave the United Way $500,000 and another $500,000 to the United Jewish Appeal. I donated the same amounts four years ago. And, three years ago, since I did very well in the stock market, I contributed $750,000 to each. Last year business was good again, so the two charities each got a million dollars."

146

Directions: Will Mildred and Benny be found? Write your answer on the lines below.

_____

_____

_____

_____

_____

_____

_____

_____

The Tao and Jewish Mothers

The Tao has no expectations. The Tao demands nothing of others. The Tao does not speak. The Tao does not blame. The Tao does not take sides. The Tao is not a Jewish mother.

Answers

True/False: Every answer is true. Jewish mothers worry about everything on the list. And more.

Essay: Benny and Mildred will be found. Here's why: It's time for the charities' annual fund drives. They'll find Mildred and her wallet . . .

You Just Can't Win

Here's a true admonition from Amy Losi's beloved Jewish mother:

When my mother would disapprove of something that I did or said, she would always say, "You'll never understand until you're a mother." As an adult—when we would disagree on how to raise my own children, she would often add, "You'll never understand until you're a grandmother." I guess I could never catch up.

See? Even more to worry about. You're always behind the eight ball.

CHAPTER 11

Expert Level

You may have noticed that I have a Ph.D.
I earned that diploma on my wall after eight
years of hard work. My Ph.D. in Jewish mother
guilt, in contrast, was a piece of cake:
It came as part of my birthright.

In previous chapters, you mastered the importance of guilt, education, unconditional love, endless food, and worry to being an effective Jewish mother. Now we're into gold medal territory for a Jewish mother: advocacy. Jewish mothers take a stand. They speak up. They right the wrongs. They go where others dare not go.

It all starts with the primacy of your child. The following Jewish mother haiku expresses it well:

Our youngest daughter,
Our most precious jewel.
Hence the name, Tiffany.

But first, let's start with a review of the basics of Jewish motherness. I want to make sure you're all set for the expert level. Take the following quiz to check your mastery of Jewish motherness.

Ten-Second Yiddish

Schlep is a Yiddish verb that means "drag around." You'd use it like this: "We had to schlep our suitcases from the dock to the cruise ship because they weighed so much that the porters couldn't lift them."

150

Use It or Lose It

Part 1: True/False

Directions: Circle *true* or *false* for each statement.

1 Actress Amanda Peet is Jewish and as of this writing, expecting her first child. Thus, she will soon be a Jewish mother.

    True   False

2 Football player Lyle Alzado (1949–1992) was Jewish. Not a Jewish mother, however.

    True   False

3 Tart TV personality Judge Judy (Judith Sheindlin, former New York family court judge) is a Jewish mother.

    True   False

4 Lemony Snicket, pseudonym for the writer of *A Series of Unfortunate Events*, is Jewish. Thus, he has a Jewish mother.

    True   False

5 The actor Yaphet Kotto from the show *Homicide* is Jewish. So is his mother.

    True   False

Part 2: Multiple Choice

Directions: Circle the letter of the correct choice.

6 The title of this book, *The Portable Jewish Mother*, is a contradiction because Jewish mothers

    A. don't need books on mothering; after all, they are the prototype for the ubermother.

    B. rarely carry things around; they have their husbands schlep things from place to place.

    C. are a unique breed: there is no other mother in the world like a Jewish mother, portable or not.

    D. usually aren't portable; they prefer to just sit quietly where they are, so they shouldn't be a bother already.

7 To most Jews, the fact of being Jewish passes from

    A. father to child

    B. potato pancake to matzoh ball to child

    C. child to mother

    D. mother to child

8 The soccer team at Vassar College is largely Jewish—although the school isn't—because

    A. everyone at Vassar recognizes that soccer is the best sport of all.

    B. Vassar is a demanding school so the kids need a way to relieve the pressure.

C. Jewish kids have always gravitated toward soccer rather than studying.

D. Jewish mothers won't let their sons play football so they join the soccer team.

9 Read this Jewish mother advice:

Drink tea and nourish life.
With the first sip, joy.
With the second sip, satisfaction.
With the third sip . . .

How would a Jewish mother complete this advice?

A. give a little burp.

B. burn your tongue.

C. fix the bathroom sink.

D. nosh on some Danish.

10 A Jewish mother shows love with

A. food

B. hugs

C. kisses

D. all of the above

Part 3: Short Answer
Directions: What is a Jewish sweater?

_____

_____

Part 4: Essay
Directions: Three Jewish mothers are sitting on a bench at a Boca Raton shopping center talking about (what else?) how much their sons love them. How does the conversation go? Write your answer on a separate piece of paper.

Answers
Part 1: True/False: Every answer is true.

Part 2: Multiple Choice: Every answer is D.

Part 3: Short Answer: See answer on page 155.

Part 4: Sample Essay

Three Jewish mothers are sitting on a bench at a Boca Raton shopping center talking about (what else?) how much their sons love them.

Sadie says, "You know the Chagall painting hanging in my living room? My son Arnold bought that for me for my seventy-fifth birthday. What a good boy he is and how much he loves his mother."

Minnie says, "You call that love? You know the Mercedes I just got for Mother's Day? That's from my son Bernie. What a doll."

Shirley says, "That's nothing. You know my son Stanley? He's in analysis with a psychoanalyst on Madison Avenue. Five sessions a week. And what does he talk about? Me."

Q: *What is a Jewish sweater?*

A: *It's a sweater that a Jewish mother puts on her child when she's cold herself.*

Yaphet Kotto

Kotto is an observant religious Jew. Born in Cameroon, he immigrated to America with his parents. Being black and Jewish made bullying inevitable, Kotto recalls. He commented to *South Coast Today* newspaper: "Going to shul, putting a yarmulke on, and having to face people who were primarily Baptists in the Bronx meant that on Fridays I was in some heavy fistfights." He had a nice Jewish mother.

Fight for Right

To me, being called a Jewish mother is a compliment, not a derogatory statement. Jewish mothers are some of the bravest and proudest people in the world because for most of us, buildings will not be named or national parks but the legacy we leave this world is our children who we hope will grow up to be great "mensches" and make this world a better place. Shalom, Judy Klau Pace

For the Jewish mother, the Impossible Dream becomes possible. The ability to stand up for your children, other people's children—in effect, the rights of everyone—is what separates the real Jewish mothers from the Jewish mother pretenders. It's like the difference between a real muffin and a low-fat, low-sugar, low-sodium one. They may look the same, but they sure don't taste the same. This story shows how to advocate for your child:

A Jewish lady's grandson is playing in the water while she is standing on the beach watching him like a hawk. Suddenly, a huge wave appears from nowhere and crashes directly over the spot where the boy is wading. The water recedes and the boy is no longer there. He has simply vanished. She holds her hands to the sky, screams, and cries,

"Lord, how could you? Have I not been a wonderful grandmother? Have I not been a wonderful mother? Have I not

lit candles every Friday night at sunset? Have I not tried my very best to live a life that you would be proud of?"

A loud voice booms from the sky, "OKAY, OKAY!" A few minutes later another huge wave appears out of nowhere and crashes on the beach. As the water recedes, the boy is standing there, smiling, splashing around as if nothing had ever happened.

The loud voice booms again "I HAVE RETURNED YOUR GRANDSON. ARE YOU SATISFIED NOW?

She responds, "He had a hat."

Two Jewish Mothers Who Advocated for Us All

Jewish mothers don't claim that their children are always right; rather, we claim that our job is to stand up for them in this cold, cruel world. But we don't limit our advocacy to children alone. True Jewish mothers take a stand against all injustice and inequality. This facet of being a Jewish mother is exemplified in the life and work of Betty Friedan and Bella Abzug.

Betty Friedan

Born Bettye Naomi Goldstein in Peoria, Illinois, in 1921, Friedan made history in 1963 when she published *The Feminine Mystique*. This landmark sociological study traces the difficulty that many women of the time faced because they were expected to fulfill themselves not through their own accomplishments, but rather by living through those of their husbands and children. *The Feminine Mystique* was one of the sparks that ignited the feminist revolution. Reviewers called it "a landmark, groundbreaking classic." A national bestseller, *The Feminine Mystique* sold well over one million copies. And Betty managed to make history while raising three children.

The Feminine Mystique launched the Second Wave of the feminist movement. In addition, Friedan also helped found the National Organization for Women, convened the National Women's Political Caucus, and was a key leader in the struggle for passage of the Equal Rights Amendment.

Nonetheless, *The New York Times'* obituary for Friedan noted that she was "famously abrasive" and that she could be "thin-skinned and imperious, subject to screaming fits of temperament." Fellow feminists echoed this sentiment, but understood that it was the key to Friedan's success:

In a 2006 essay in *The Guardian*, Germaine Greer wrote:

> *Betty Friedan changed the course of human history almost single-handedly. Her ex-husband, Carl Friedan, believes this; Betty believed it too. This belief was the key to a good deal of Betty's behavior; she would become breathless with outrage if she didn't*

The Portable Jewish Mother

get the deference she thought she deserved. Though her behavior was often tiresome, I figured that she had a point. Women don't get the respect they deserve unless they are wielding male-shaped power; if they represent women they will be called "love" and expected to clear up after themselves. Betty wanted to change that forever.

Betty Friedan was a courageous Jewish mother who fought for all people, not just her own three children. As such, she's a model for all Jewish mothers who advocate for right.

"Battling Bella" Abzug

Bella Savitsky Abzug, born in 1920, was a well-known American politician and a leader of the women's movement. Never one to back down from a righteous cause, Abzug herself said, "I was born yelling." She was raised in the Bronx, New York, by poor Russian Jewish immigrants. By the age of thirteen, Abzug was already giving speeches and defying convention at the local synagogue. Forbidden by tradition from saying Kaddish, the Hebrew prayer for the dead, for her father, she did so anyway. In so doing, she learned a valuable lesson that guided her life: "Be bold, be brazen, be true to your heart." Abzug was student government president at Hunter College and attended Columbia Law School on a scholarship.

Perhaps best known for her famous remark, "This woman's place is in the House—the House of Representatives," Abzug ran a successful 1970 campaign to join that body. She was re-elected three times. By being extremely outspoken, combative, tough, and determined, Abzug achieved splendid victories for women. These include:

* Initiating the Congressional caucus on women's issues.
* Organizing the National Women's Political Caucus.
* Serving as chief strategist for the Democratic Women's Committee (achieving equal representation for women in all elective and appointive posts, including presidential conventions).
* Writing the first law banning discrimination against women in obtaining credit, credit cards, loans, and mortgages.
* Introducing pioneering bills on comprehensive child care, Social Security for homemakers, family planning, and abortion rights.
* Introducing an amendment to the Civil Rights Act to include gay and lesbian rights.
* Last, but certainly most important: raising two daughters.

In a 1977 Gallup poll, Abzug was named one of the twenty most influential women of the world. Republican Millicent Fenwick once said that Abzug was one of her heroes because she had vast integrity, spoke from the heart, and spoke the truth to people in power. In 1998, Abzug delivered her last public speech, dying shortly after. She is sorely missed.

She advised others to do what was right to make the world a better place. She said: "People may not like it, but no one will stop you." They sure didn't stop Bella.

Like Betty Friedan, Bella Abzug was a brave Jewish mother who battled for all people, not just her own two daughters. She's another exemplary role model for all Jewish mothers who take a stand.

The Squeaky Wheel Gets the Oil

Have you heard the following Jewish mother joke?

> *A Jewish man is lying on the operating table, about to be operated on by his son, the surgeon. The father says, "Son, think of it this way . . . If anything happens to me, your mother is coming to live with you."*

When the Jewish mother stands up for her kiddies or demands social change, she is often

criticized as being aggressive and over-bearing. By stating what she thinks and doing what she knows is right, the Jewish mother inspires fear: After all, who does she think she is? Perhaps most frightening of all, she doesn't fit into the neat package of traditional American womanhood—the old-fashioned sitcom mother with the sweet smile and twin sweater set.

History bears this out. As scholar Phyllis Chesler says, "Like women of color, Jewish women in the nineteenth century were considered too pushy, crude, and not ladylike. They were all elbows akimbo, not well-dressed, vulgar, and often cheap."

But black mothers are usually given respect and Jewish mothers are often mocked and stereotyped.

And she can't win either way: When she refuses to assert herself, the Jewish mother becomes the martyr, a mistress of passive aggression. This joke sums up this aspect of the stereotype:

A Jewish woman decides to prepare her will and make her final requests. She says to her rabbi, "I have two final requests. First, I want to be cremated, and second, I want my ashes scattered all over the shopping mall."

"Why the shopping mall?" asks the rabbi.

"Then I'll be sure my daughters visit me twice a week."

As my colleague and friend Dr. Ann Shapiro said: "Alas, I can't think of any witty comments about being a Jewish mother, which I regard as a life sentence. I'm not sure whether there is any time off for good behavior." Ann feels that way because, as with many Jewish mothers, she is still helping her children find their path in life. A stereotypical Jewish mother never stops helping.

To Boldly Go Where No One Has Gone Before

But the qualities that Jewish mother jokes ridicule—a Jewish mother's assertive stance as well as her staunch support of her children, her friends, and her social causes—are actually sources of considerable pride. All too often, you have to be demanding and insistent to effect change, especially when it comes to women. Someone has to step in and improve the status quo. People pleasers rarely get the job done because they're too busy trying to win popularity contests.

We see this with the number of Jewish politicians, both men and women, who have made the world a better place. Women who complain that something is wrong are usually the same women who make things a whole lot better for the rest of us.

In the following quiz, match each female Jewish politician with her leadership role and accomplishments.

Jewish Mother Movers and Shakers

Jewish Politician	Famous Role/Achievement
Bella Abzug	
Barbara Boxer	
Kitty Dukakis	
Dianne Feinstein	
Susan Golding	
Florence Kahn	
Vera Katz	
Madeleine Kunin	
Linda Lingle	
Sophie Masloff	

The American Jewess

The American Jewess, published for only four years (1895–1899), nonetheless left a significant historical mark. Characterizing itself as "the only magazine in the world devoted to the interests of Jewish women," *The American Jewess* hit a wide range of topics, from religion to recreation.

Jewish Politician	Famous Role/Achievement
Bella Abzug	Feminist leader and gay rights activist (D-NY: 1971–77)
Barbara Boxer	Senator (D-CA: 1992–) Boxer has been a vocal advocate for environmental issues, women's rights, gun control, and medical research.
Kitty Dukakis	Served as a member of the U.S. Holocaust Memorial Council and the President's Commission on the Holocaust; wife of 1988 presidential candidate Michael Dukakis
Dianne Feinstein	San Francisco's first (and to date, only) female mayor; senator (D-CA: 1992–)
Susan Golding	San Diego mayor (1992–2000)
Florence Kahn	First Jewish woman U.S. representative (R-CA: 1925–37)
Vera Katz	Portland, Oregon, mayor (1992–2004)
Madeleine Kunin	Governor of Vermont (1985–91)
Linda Lingle	Governor of Hawaii (2002–)
Sophie Masloff	Pittsburgh mayor (1988–93)

Turnabout Is Fair Play

I don't want to be accused of being unfair to men, so below is a list of famous male Jewish politicians. See if you can match each male Jewish politician with his leadership role and accomplishments. Remember: Each of these accomplished men was raised by a Jewish mother.

Male Jewish Movers and Shakers

Name	Accomplishment
Judah Benjamin	
Michael Bloomberg	
Barney Frank	
Kinky Friedman	
Henry Kissinger	
Fiorello LaGuardia	
Lewis Charles Levin	
Joseph Lieberman	
Robert Reich	
Francis Salvador	
Charles Schumer	
Oscar Straus	

Answers

Name	Accomplishment
Judah Benjamin	Confederate attorney general (1861), secretary of war (1861), and secretary of state (1862–65)
Michael Bloomberg	New York City mayor (2002–)
Barney Frank	Openly gay politician (D-MA: 1981–)
Kinky Friedman	2006 Texas Independent gubernatorial candidate
Henry Kissinger	National security adviser (1969–75), secretary of state (1973–77)
Fiorello LaGuardia	New York City mayor (1934–45). (He had a Jewish mother.)
Lewis Charles Levin	First Jewish U.S. representative (PA: 1845–51)
Joseph Lieberman	Vice-presidential candidate on 2000 Democratic Party ticket with presidential candidate Al Gore. The first Jewish candidate for vice president.
Robert Reich	Secretary of labor (1993–97)
Francis Salvador	First Jewish member of a colonial legislature
Charles Schumer	Senator (D-NY: 1999–)
Oscar Straus	Secretary of commerce and labor (1906–09)

Expert Level

Kinky Friedman and the Texas Jewboys

Richard S. "Kinky" Friedman is a singer, songwriter, novelist, politician, and former columnist for *Texas Monthly*. When I started this book, Kinky was running for governor of Texas. When I finished, Kinky had lost. Alas! He didn't make history by becoming the first Jewish governor of Texas. But we know that Kinky's mother is proud of her boychick anyway for fighting the good fight.

Jewish Mothers of Valor

Many of the Jewish women I surveyed admired their mothers tremendously, especially for their support and advocacy. These women ignored the stereotype of the Jewish mother to embrace the truth: Many Jewish mothers inspire, support, and lavish love.

Role Model #1

Here's what my close friend Dorrie Berkowitz said about her mother:

While my mother was not the stereotypical Jewish mother (radical feminist, sailor's vocabulary!), she was indeed the quintessential Jewish grandmother. Her grandchildren were not only geniuses, but also angels. No matter that we, their parents, were

The Portable Jewish Mother

banging our heads against the wall. According to Grandma, they were perfect, and should not be denied any request. Grandma was the one who allowed the consumption of an entire bag of mini-Reese's Peanut Butter Cups. (Never mind that they came back up at home at 2:00 the following morning.) Grandma was the one who purchased the special pump to go in the Fox's U-Bet jar of chocolate syrup that was always in her refrigerator. (God forbid the evil parents should make such a frivolous purchase.) Her children never doubted that she loved us unconditionally and would defend us to the death; her grandchildren, however, were fortunate to experience the Land of Oz, ruled over by Grandma. We miss her, every one.

Role Model #2

My longtime friend Jodi Saviuk places the notion of female Jewish advocacy in a slightly different light. Jodi is one of those people who always makes things just a little bit better by her support and common sense. She wrote:

I am a Jewish mother, I had a Jewish mother, and I know many Jewish mothers, so what can I say? Maybe the only two real things I believe in and try to tell my kids about Life is that some things are meant to be, and that you should always strive to be "a mensch," an honorable person, someone who tries to do the right thing.

Role Model #3

Pessha Snedecker stumbled on my name on the spine of a book, started reading my oeuvre, and has become my loyal and supportive fan—and my friend. We spent a wild afternoon a few years ago racing around Las Vegas in her Beemer. Here's what she said about her Jewish mother's unending support and strength:

My license plate read "LUCKI MI." I had the world's greatest mother. My mother, widowed when I was 8 during the Depression (1931), with no marketable skills, took two jobs. In the day time, she demonstrated a brand new product—Bisquick—in grocery stores. In the evening, she took tickets in a movie box office. This was before Social Security, of course. Catholic charities placed "elderly" women in homes to care for the children of working mothers in exchange for room, board and $3.00 a week.

Our "elderly caregiver" was 65 (I'm now 83).

I lacked for nothing. I was introduced to music (piano lessons and ballet), enrolled in what was called Children's Concerts at Orchestra Hall in Chicago. Every Wednesday afternoon I was allowed to leave school and take the bus downtown. I was taken to museums to learn about art. I was well dressed and never felt deprived. We celebrated Jewish holidays, went to Temple and Sunday school.

The Portable Jewish Mother

I'm so proud of my Jewish heritage that I still fast on Yom Kippur, eat matzohs on Pesach, and burn Yahrzeit candles to remind me whence I came.

In the next chapter, we'll explore the minefield that is Jewish marriage—especially when it comes to your children deciding that they want to get married.

CHAPTER 12

Getting Your Kids Married

Why the emphasis on getting our adult children to walk down the aisle, say "I do," and step on the glass? Find out in this chapter.

A Jewish mother's work is never done. We birth 'em, we feed 'em, we chauffeur 'em, and then we have to make sure they marry the right person. After all, if the Jewish mother doesn't take charge of this essential task, who will? (And if someone else does, you can bet that it won't be done right.) Sigh.

Judaism considers marriage to be the ideal state of existence; a man without a wife, or a woman without a husband, is considered incomplete. After all, Genesis says "Be fruitful and multiply" (1:28). Traditionally, a man who remained unmarried after age twenty was considered cursed by God. He was living without blessing or happiness. Thus, a true Jewish mother stereotype devotes herself to making sure that her children marry—and marry well.

Another factor is that Jews tend to marry later, and have more education and a lower birthrate than the rest of Americans. On average, Jewish women have fewer than two children each, too few to replace the Jewish population. These challenges deserve the attention of the Jewish mother. Thank goodness we're up to the task.

Never Good Enough?
According to the stereotype, almost no young woman is good enough for a Jewish mother's son. And few men are good enough for a Jewish mother's daughter. Here's an example:

Sylvia was telling Myrtle about her kids. She said, "My daughter married such a nice man. A real mensch. He lets her sleep late; she doesn't get up until noon. She eats breakfast in bed and doesn't do any housework. Oh, what a life he's given her. But my son . . .

"Oy, did he marry badly! She's such a chazzer! She stays in bed all day; she doesn't get up before noon. She eats breakfast in bed and doesn't do any housework. This is a wife?"

Nothing like a good double standard, eh? After all, the Jewish mother has devoted her life to raising her children. This has entailed significant sacrifice and self-denial. So she should let her child settle for anything less than the perfect mate? I think not.

The following joke sums up the stereotype of Jewish mothers and their sons' marriages:

A young Jewish man excitedly tells his mother he's fallen in love and is going to get married. He says, "Just for fun, Ma, I'm going to bring over three women and you try to guess which one I'm going to marry." The mother agrees.

The next day, he brings three beautiful women to meet her. They sit and chat. He then says, "Okay, Ma. Which one am I marrying?"

She immediately replies, "The redhead in the middle."

Shocked, the young man replies, "That's amazing, Ma. You're right. How did you know?"

The Jewish mother replies, "I don't like her."

Picky, Picky

Are Jewish mothers really that picky when it comes to their child's choice of a mate? Do Jewish mothers really meddle that much in their children's love lives? I polled my friends to find out. Take the following test to compare your perceptions with their reality. (I admit my friends could be biased, but they've got years of experience in the field.)

You Call It "Meddling"; We Call It "Concern"

Part 1: Multiple Choice
Directions: Circle the letter of the correct choice.

What percentage of Jewish mothers . . .
1. meddle when their children date?
   A. 10 percent
   B. 25 percent
   C. 50 percent
2. question their children about whether or not they're dating?
   A. 10 percent
   B. 20 percent
   C. 40 percent

3 want their children to find a date at the synagogue rather than, say, the local bar?
- A. 10 percent
- B. 25 percent
- C. 35 percent

4 ask about their children's sex life?
- A. 0 percent
- B. 20 percent
- C. 40 percent

5 criticize the people their children date?
- A. 3 percent
- B. 17 percent
- C. 25 percent

6 search online sites to find their children a date?
- A. 1 percent
- B. 5 percent
- C. 10 percent

Part 2: Essay

Directions: What happens when a gay Jewish boy announces that he's found a girl he wants to marry? Write your answer on a separate piece of paper.

The Portable Jewish Mother

Answers

Part 1: Multiple Choice: Every answer is C.

Part 2: Sample Essay:

A gay Jewish boy phones home, and says, "Mama, I know I told you that I'm gay, but I've met a wonderful girl and we're going to be married. I know this will come as a huge relief to you, as my gay lifestyle had been a source of much distress for you."

"Such wonderful news, my baby," his mother chortles in her joy. "I'll start making wedding plans immediately! Then after a pause, she ventures, "I suppose it's too much to hope that the girl is also Jewish?"

He replies, "Yes, Momma, she is Jewish. And what's more, she's from a very wealthy and respectable Beverly Hills family."

Mama is beside herself! "And what is the name of this wonderful girl?" she asks.

And the son replies, "Monica Lewinsky." There is a long pause. Then Mama asks, "Whatever happened to that nice black boy you were dating last year?"

> *To keep your marriage brimming,*
> *With love in the loving cup,*
> *Whenever you're wrong, admit it;*
> *Whenever you're right, shut up.*

—Ogden Nash

Be Proactive

So, should a Jewish mother meddle in her child's love life? Should she choose the proper partner? Should she work to get her child married? Of course she should. After all, she's the expert. And to make it easy for you, just follow these easy steps:

1. Let your child choose his or her own mate. If this does not occur by the time the child is eighteen months old, step in.
2. Survey all your friends and relatives. See who has a promising young man or woman coming up through the ranks.
3. Accost total strangers in movie theaters, Broadway plays, and restaurants, too. Just because it's dark and quiet and people are trying to concentrate on other things should not keep you from approaching them and asking if they know any nice young Jewish men.
4. Point out the happiness that marriage can bring. (This is not the time to refer to your husband as "That putz I married.")
5. Judge all prospects closely. I've provided a worksheet to help you with this essential task.
6. Don't hesitate to listen in on your child's phone conversations and hack their e-mail. It's vital to be informed about their love life.
7. Automatically assume that you'll hate anyone that you did not choose. After all, better safe than sorry.

8. Come up with clever excuses to eliminate prospects you don't like. Possibilities include "He's too tall, short, fat, thin, old, young, rich, poor, stupid, educated, religious, not religious, hairy, etc."

9. Make your child's life as miserable as possible. It's only through misery that he can know the true happiness of a good marriage.

10. If necessary, take your fifty-year-old son with you when you play mahjong. There are lots of nice marriageable prospects at such events. In a pinch, the book club will do, too. He will feel very comfortable among your friends.

Marriageable Prospects Worksheet

Make many copies of this worksheet and have one with you at all times. Be sure to carry a pen, too. Whip out a worksheet when you spot a live prospect. As you ask questions, fill in the worksheet. If the stranger asks, "What ARE you doing?" Don't hesitate to respond, "I'm trying to find my son/daughter a wife/husband. Now, you said you were single and went to Princeton, yes?"

Marriageable Prospects Worksheet

1 Do you love your mother more than anyone else in the world?
_____

2 Are you Jewish? _____

3 Are you straight? (or gay, depending on your needs) _____

4 Did you attend Hebrew school? _____

5 Were your teeth straightened? _____

6 Did you take music lessons? (violin for a boy, piano for a girl)
_____

7 How well do you do in school? (Immediately cross off anyone who does not have a 4.0 grade point average, unless there's a trust fund involved.) _____

8 What college did you graduate from? (Give 10 extra points for an Ivy League graduate.) _____

9 When do you expect your medical or law degree? _____

10 What makes your mother so wonderful? _____
_____

11 What is your yearly salary? _____

12 When do you anticipate making partner? _____

180

The Portable Jewish Mother

Never Give Up

If, after all your hard work, your son still chooses someone unsuitable, make every effort to make her life miserable. For instance, refer to her in the Third-Person Invisible, as in "Is She still here?" Butt into their lives early and often. Here are some additional suggestions. They're all easy and effective.

* Criticize your daughter-in-law every chance you get. Attack her housekeeping and parenting style. Be sure to speak as loudly as possible so everyone in the restaurant can hear.

* Bring over meals, because it's plain that She isn't feeding your son.

* Clean her house, because it's bound to be filthy. If you're not into cleaning, hire someone to do it. You can also rearrange the furniture. Daughters-in-law love this.

* Show up at their house as often as you can. Never announce your visit.

* Remember all slights and minor offenses. Bring them up often, especially at large family meals.

* Try a little sabotage. For instance, give your daughter-in-law the recipe for your son's favorite matzoh balls. Then leave out the crucial ingredient—matzoh meal.

* If all else fails, actively work to undermine the marriage.

Gay Children

Just because your child is gay doesn't mean that you refrain from meddling in his or her love life. It simply means that you have a smaller pool of applicants from which to choose. Thus, you must work harder to find The One.

Of course, you'd never follow my tongue-in-cheek suggestions. You would never meddle in your child's love life. Right. But as you meddle, remember to be gentle. Like guilt, a little meddling goes a very looooooooooooong way.

Matchmaker, Matchmaker, Make Me a Match

"My Jewish mother is such a matchmaker. She's always trying to find me a date," you complain. "Where does she get off meddling in my love life?" Not so fast: Matchmaking has a long and respected heritage in many cultures, especially in the Jewish community. There's nothing new about it at all. And as you'll read later in this chapter, many adult children welcome their mothers taking an active role in finding them a spouse.

In the Middle Ages, Catholic priests also lent a hand when it came to matchmaking. In frontier North America, line dances and square dances were often used for matchmaking. Matchmakers, acting as formal chaperones or as self-employed freelancers, would attend these events and scout out prospects—as well as report on any developing romances. This shows you that matchmaking was not unique to Jewish mothers, not by a long shot.

In Jewish culture, the role of the matchmaker is quite professionalized. In traditional Jewish communities, rabbis were expected to serve as matchmakers.

The Ashkenazi Jewish *shadchen* was often regarded as an essential adviser when it came to arranging a marriage.

The Shadchen and the Shidduch

The *shadchen* (SHOD-khen) is a professional matchmaker. The term is also used for anyone who brings together a man and a woman that results in a wedding, but a professional shadchen often gets a fee for his or her services. The *shidduch* (SHID-dakh) is an arranged marriage.

Jewish marriages were traditionally arranged by the heads of two families. The shadchen had the following tasks:

* Gather information about potential mates.
* Assess each person's level of religious observance.
* Investigate family backgrounds.
* Consider the qualities of the potential bride and/or groom.
* Match personality traits.

Among some Orthodox Jews, dating is only allowed when people are actively searching for a marriage partner. Dating occurs after both sides make inquiries about the prospective partner. After the match has been proposed, the prospective partners see each other a number of times to discover whether or not they get along. The number of times a couple meets before a decision has to be made whether to get engaged or not depends on the community practice.

Online Dating

Everyone's heard of Internet dating services (and you may have even tried them). They're constantly advertised on the radio, television, newspapers, and magazines. And all that advertising is paying off: Americans spent nearly $470 million on online dating and personals in 2004, the largest segment of "paid content" on the Web, according to a study conducted by the Online Publishers Association (OPA) and comScore Networks, Inc. At the end of November 2004, there were 844 lifestyle and dating sites, a 38 percent increase since the start of the year, according to Hitwise Inc.

People seeking dates provide personal information, then search for other individuals using criteria such as age range, gender, sexual orientation, religion, and geographical location. On most Web sites, members can post their photographs. This would be useless, of course, unless they could check out all the other photos—which they can. In addition, some sites offer additional technological matchmaking, including online chats, message boards, and Webcasts. In most cases, fees are assessed.

Yenta

Yenta is the Yiddish word for "matchmaker." Today, the term has come to mean a meddler, gossiper, and busybody. You'd use it like this: "That yenta is always butting into my life and trying to get me to marry her nephew Sheldon."

JDate.com

Some young Jewish singles may have hoped that online dating companies would do away with their mother's matchmaking. But no dice. JDate.com—the biggest online Jewish dating network, with 52,500 members in the New York area alone—has seen just the opposite effect. Computer-savvy Jewish mothers are using JDate to find dates for their adult children. How? They just log on and pretend to be their children!

Predictably, most children are less than delighted to find their mothers trolling the Net for a rich Jewish doctor, lawyer, or Indian chief for them. Every once in a while, the gambit pays off when a match is made. Then the Jewish mother can smugly rest on her laurels and retire her JDate subscription.

Ironically, the difficulties with online dating services has created a return to the role of the traditional professional matchmaker. Those who find dating systems or services useful but prefer human intelligence and personal touches can choose from a wide range of such services now available.

Marriage and Judaism

So your daughter has finally found someone who passes muster. They plan to marry. Perhaps the encounter goes like this:

A nice Jewish girl brings home her fiancé to meet her parents. After dinner, her mother tells her father to find out about the young man. He invites the fiancé to his study for schnapps.

"So what are your plans?" the father asks the fiancé.

"I am a Torah scholar," he replies.

"A Torah scholar," the father says. "Admirable, but what will you do to provide a nice house for my daughter to live in, as she's accustomed to?"

"I will study," the young man replies, "and God will provide for us."

"And how will you buy her a beautiful engagement ring, such as she deserves?" asks the father.

"I will concentrate on my studies," the young man replies, "God will provide for us."

The Portable Jewish Mother

> "And children?" asks the father. "How will you support children?"
>
> "Don't worry, sir. God will provide," replies the fiancé.
>
> The conversation goes on like this, and each time the father questions, the fiancé insists that God will provide.
>
> Later, the mother asks, "So nu? How did it go?"
>
> The father answers, "He has no job and no plans, but the good news is he thinks I'm God."

To Jews, as with nearly everyone else, marriage is an extremely important life-cycle event. Secular Jewish marriages and religious Jewish marriages are not the same. Let's start with secular Jewish marriages. In America, as with many other countries, the couple must obtain a civil license before being married by anyone. A rabbi, therefore, cannot legally officiate at a wedding ceremony unless the couple has obtained a civil license. Then we have the religious Jewish marriage. In this case, the civil license is secondary because some rabbis won't officiate at interfaith marriages. Now, you plan the wedding. Two especially interesting aspects to consider are the ketubah and the chuppah.

The Ketubah

Among observant Jews, the wedding event starts with a *ketubah*, the legal Jewish document that lays out a wife's rights and a husband's obligations. It's a remarkable document because it's so far-seeing. Below are the rights and obligations the ketubah provides:

The Marriage Contract

Wife's Rights	Husband's Obligations
Receive monetary payments upon termination of the marriage by death or divorce	Provide food Provide shelter Provide clothing Provide sexual satisfaction to the wife

Orthodox Judaism uses a traditional ketubah based on the forms that have evolved and standardized over the past millennium.

The Chuppah

Chuppah (KHU-peh) is also spelled *huppa*, *chupah*, or *chuppa*. It's a canopy traditionally used in Jewish weddings. It's used in nearly all Orthodox and Conservative marriages and some Reform ones. You learned about the division of Judaism in earlier chapters.

The chuppah consists of an embroidered cloth stretched or supported over four poles. Usually made of white silk or satin, it

188

can also be a prayer shawl. It may be embroidered with a biblical quotation. Sometimes, the chuppah is held aloft by male relatives; other times, it's fixed to the ground. In all instances, the couple stands under it as they take their vows.

The chuppah symbolizes the home that the couple will build together. This "home" is initially devoid of furniture as a reminder that the basis of a Jewish home is the people within it, not the possessions.

The chuppah isn't unique to Jewish marriages; neither did the Jews invent it. The Greeks use a variation of the chuppah; so do Indian Brahmans. There are other cultures with the same tradition as well.

Interfaith Marriage

Intermarriage is a serious issue to the Jewish mother. Before we get into the seriousness, enjoy this humorous look at intermarriage:

The devout Jew was beside himself because his son had been dating a shiksa, so he went to visit his rabbi. The rabbi listened solemnly to his problem, took his hand, and said, "Pray to God."

So the Jew went to the synagogue, bowed his head, and prayed, "God, please help me. My son, my favorite son, he's going to marry a shiksa, he sees nothing but goyim . . ."

"Your son," boomed a voice down from the heavens. *"You think you got problems? What about my son?"*

Today, about 40 percent of all Jews marry non-Jews. Before 1970, fewer than 15 percent of Jews married non-Jews. According to the recent National Jewish Population Survey, not only is the number of Jews who marry non-Jews rising in the last decade, but two-thirds of the children of interfaith couples are not being raised as Jews. In contrast, close to 100 percent of the children of Jewish couples are raised as Jews.

The survey also found that the Jewish population in the United States as a whole fell in numbers and aged in the past ten years. There are about 300,000 fewer Jews in America in the last decade, despite recent Jewish immigrants from the former Soviet Union.

All branches of Orthodox Judaism refuse to accept the validity of intermarriages. Reform Judaism and Reconstructionist Judaism take intermarriage on a case-by-case basis. Therefore, many Reform and Reconstructionist rabbis will officiate at a marriage between a Jew and a gentile, as long as the couple agrees to certain conditions. These conditions usually state that the couple must raise the children as Jewish and provide them with some sort of formal Jewish education.

Jewish Marriage Statistics

Jews marry later than other Americans, with the greatest disparities occurring in the age group between twenty-five and thirty-four. For Jewish women in particular, late marriage means lower rates of fertility compared with other Caucasian women—who themselves are barely producing babies at replacement level. At no point do Jewish women attain the fertility levels of their non-Jewish peers or bear children in numbers sufficient to offset population losses from natural causes.

When Things Don't Work Out: Jewish Divorce

Halacha (Jewish law) allows for divorce. A religious (as distinguished from a civil) divorce terminates a marriage between Orthodox Jews. A divorce can take place only if husband and wife both agree to it and if the civil courts have already granted a civil divorce.

The document of divorce is termed a *get*. The final divorce ceremony involves the husband giving the get document to the ex-wife or her agent, but the wife may sue in rabbinical court to initiate the divorce. If a man refuses to grant his wife a divorce, she cannot remarry religiously until the divorce is granted. As a general rule, Reform rabbis do not ask for a religious divorce in addition to a civil one.

In Chapter 13, you'll learn how to raise a Jewish child. I'm assuming that you understand that your function on earth, once you're married, is to reproduce. A traditional Jewish mother expects at least two grandchildren.

How to Raise a Jewish Child

(In Case You Slept Through Hebrew School)

How do you raise a Jewish child? The same way you raise any child: with a lot of love, food, guilt, and Jewish customs and traditions. OK, so maybe it isn't the same after all.

The following comment came from Professor Barbara Bengels, a very close friend whom everyone identifies as a classic Jewish mother. She has all the qualities: the worry and the warmth, the emphasis on education and the extremely accomplished daughters, the abundance of food and desire to feed the world. You'd think she was raised steeped in Jewish customs. And you would be wrong. Completely wrong. Here's what she wrote to me:

> *My problem: I had the most goyish mother imaginable. She didn't even know she was Jewish until my younger brother Michael was born (which was ten years after I was born). But somehow I inherited the Guilt Factor nonetheless . . .*

Not to the Manor Born

As this comment shows, being a Jewish mother doesn't mean you were raised in an observant Jewish household. Far from it. In fact, many Jewish mothers were raised in highly secular homes, especially those children raised in the 1950s and 1960s, when their parents, highly aware of anti-Semitism, tried to blend into the mainstream. Many people in this generation gave their children "American" names, fed them "American" foods, and taught them English rather than Yiddish. Nonetheless, these children absorbed some Jewish mother values through osmosis, especially the importance of having children of their own.

Below are some of the other lessons that got transmitted through the atmosphere in a Jewish home. How many of them did *your* Jewish mother teach you?

Instant Yiddish

Kinder is the German and Yiddish word for "children." It is always said with enormous pride, especially by Jewish mothers. (Little children are *kinderlach*.)

Things I Know That I Didn't Learn in Hebrew School

1. The High Holy Days have absolutely nothing to do with marijuana.
2. Where there's smoke, there may be salmon.
3. No meal is complete without leftovers.
4. According to Jewish dietary law, pork and shellfish may be eaten only in Chinese restaurants.
5. A *shmata* (Yiddish for "rag") is a dress that your husband's ex is wearing.
6. You need ten men for a minion, but only four in polyester pants and white shoes for pinochle.

7. One mitzvah can change the world; two will just make you tired.

8. Anything worth saying is worth repeating a thousand times.

9. Never take a front-row seat at a bris.

10. Next year in Jerusalem. The year after that, how about a nice cruise?

11. Never leave a restaurant empty-handed.

12. Spring ahead, fall back, winter in Boca.

13. WASPs leave and never say goodbye; Jews say goodbye and never leave.

14. Always whisper the names of diseases.

15. If it tastes good, it's probably not kosher.

16. The important Jewish holidays are the ones on which alternate side of the street parking is suspended.

17. Laugh now, but one day you'll be driving a Lexus and eating dinner at 4:00 P.M. in Florida.

18. Without Jewish mothers, who would need therapy?

It All Starts with Kids

So you have the traditional Jewish values (especially the guilt and worry) but may not know the traditional Jewish customs. This chapter is designed to help you raise your child in the Jewish community, according to the traditions of Jewish motherhood.

Start with this immutable fact: Kids are the center of a Jewish mother's universe. I am a case in point. I earned a B.A., an M.A., and a Ph.D., all with the highest honors. I earned post-doc credits and various certificates, including one in technical writing. I've published more than 200 books and scores of articles. I've received the highest teaching award in the State University of New York, the Chancellor's Award for Excellence in Teaching. I've appeared on national television, including *Live with Regis and Kelly*, *The Maury Povich Show*, the *CBS Morning Show*, and many more. Not too shabby, eh? So what did my father say to me in light of all my professional accomplishments? "The thing that will give you the most pleasure in your life will be your children." Know what? He was right.

This is not to say that the Jewish tradition denigrates female accomplishments. Far from it. But the Jewish tradition venerates Jewish motherhood. And to be a Jewish mother, you need kids. Fortunately, the kids don't have to be your own.

For instance, you can borrow nephews and nieces. I have my own children, but I adore my niece Liz Fink and take an active role in her life. I've also mentored other children, most notably friends of my own kids.

A Jewish mother without children of her own can serve as a Big Sister. This makes her a Jewish mother. You can mentor a newcomer at work; you can volunteer for Girl Scouts. You can teach. Some of the best Jewish mothers are teachers. My daughter's third-grade teacher has mentored my daughter. This teacher isn't Jewish and doesn't have children. Nonetheless, I consider her a Jewish mother because of the advice she gives and the interest she takes in my daughter. To be a Jewish mother, you just have to make a commitment to helping children.

Children can drive you crazy, but they are the center of the world, as the following story illustrates:

> *Three Jewish women get together for lunch. As they are being seated in the restaurant, one takes a deep breath and gives a long, slow "Oy." The second takes a deep breath as well and lets out a long, slow "Oy." The third takes a deep breath and says impatiently, "Girls, I thought we agreed that we weren't going to talk about our children."*

Baby, Baby: Birth Customs

The birth of her child is the happiest day in a Jewish mother's life (and it better be the happiest day in a Jewish father's life as well, if he knows what's good for him). Observant Jews traditionally hold a bris to mark the birth of a boy. Some Jewish families hold a naming ceremony to mark the birth of a girl, but this is a relatively new custom.

Bris: Or It Won't Be Long Now

Two little Jewish baby boys are talking. We'll call them Jake and David. David says, "I'm getting operated on tomorrow."

Jake replies, "Oh? What are they going to do?"

"Circumcise me!" says David.

"I had that done when I was just a few days old," replies Jake.

"Did it hurt?" asks David.

"I couldn't walk for a year!" Jake replies.

In Hebrew, the operation to remove a baby boy's foreskin is called a *brit milah*; in Yiddish, it's called a *bris*. No matter what we call it, a bris is a Jewish religious ceremony that welcomes infant Jewish boys into a covenant between God and the children of Israel. It's usually performed eight days after the baby's birth. A circumciser called a *mohel* performs the ceremony before family and friends. In addition, the baby boy is given his Hebrew name during the ceremony. As usual, there's a nice spread after. When it comes to a Jewish custom or holiday, there's almost *always* a meal.

In Genesis 17:10, the Lord says: "This is my covenant . . . every man among you shall be circumcised." It's been my very informal and not at all scientific observation that even non-observant Jews have their sons circumcised. This is one of those ceremonies that strengthen Jewish identity and bind people to the entire Jewish community. When it comes to a bris, the role of the Jewish mother is clear: You stand there trying to look brave but secretly wondering why this has to be done to *your* adorable boychick.

Q: *If a doctor carries a black bag and a plumber carries a toolbox, what does a mohel carry?*

A: *A bris-kit.*

Naming Ceremony: Or Something for Jewish Baby Girls

There's no equivalent of a bris for girls, but some Jewish families hold a naming ceremony to welcome infant girls into the fold. This is a new "tradition," as there's nothing in the Bible to support it. The ceremony is usually held in synagogue on the first Shabbat after the baby's birth and is just what the name suggests: a ceremony in which the baby receives her Hebrew name. After, candy and other sweets are thrown to wish a sweet life for the baby and her parents. Unlike a bris, the naming ceremony doesn't cause a Jewish mother to mutter "Oy! Oy! Oy!" under her breath.

Bar Mitzvah and Bat Mitzvah

This one's like getting your driver's license: It means you're a grown-up and responsible for your actions. You're also responsible for observing the Jewish commandments—all 613 of them. This confirmation of adulthood takes place when a Jewish girl is twelve years old and a Jewish boy is thirteen years old—which proves that girls do mature faster than boys. Here's the lingo: A boy becomes bar mitzvah; a girl becomes bat mitzvah. This means the kid, not the ceremony, is the bar or bat mitzvah.

The bar mitzvah ceremony is relatively new, when we consider the ancient history of the Jewish people: It developed in medieval times. Today, most ceremonies involve the child reciting the blessings for the Torah reading, reading from the Torah, reading from the Haftorah, and giving a discussion of that week's Torah portion. The child may also lead part of the morning prayer and make a speech. The speech should always thank your Jewish mother for making you such a swell kid.

However, different divisions of Judaism celebrate differently: An Orthodox Jewish bar mitzvah is different from a Reform one, for instance. Girls didn't even have a ceremony until the twentieth century: The first public celebration of a bat mitzvah took place in 1922. Naturally, it was in New York City, that hotbed of liberalism.

Ceremony and Party Optional

Even without a ceremony, a child automatically assumes the full responsibilities of Jewish adulthood at age twelve or thirteen, depending on gender. Not having a bar or bat mitzvah celebration doesn't make a person any less of a Jew. But who wants to pass up a great party with lots of carousing, dancing, and a huge table of desserts? Besides, in thirty years, you can remind your friend Arnie Schwartz-Blumenthal that he had a *Star Wars*–themed bar mitzvah and looked like a putz in his powder blue tux, holding a light saber.

Cram Time

Typically, Jewish children prepare for their bar or bat mitzvah by studying in the synagogue in formal classes. Others get tutors at home; you can even study on your own. There's no hard-and-fast rule about this. There's no rule at all, actually. For Jewish mothers, Hebrew school invariably means carpools.

Gifts

What's a big party without gifts? Because the Hebrew word for "life," *chai*, is also the Hebrew number 18, monetary gifts in multiples of $18 ($36, $180, and so on) are considered good luck and have become very common. Never one to go with the flow, I

The Portable Jewish Mother

gave my best friend Marla Meg a puppy for her bat mitzvah. She was enchanted, but her parents were far less delighted. Dr. and Mrs. Gordon, please accept my public apology for the puppy.

According to the White House Web site, U.S. citizens can request a White House greeting from the president to commemorate a bar or bat mitzvah by sending a notice six weeks prior. The White House also sends greetings for the birth of a baby, weddings, landmark birthdays, and so on. This is assuming you like the current president, of course. If you're in denial, you can pass on this part.

In the next chapter, you'll learn to make some of the delicious foods that we eat during these celebrations and holidays. Jewish Mamas, fire up your stoves!

CHAPTER 14

How Jewish Mothers

Celebrate the Holidays

The holidays are a time of great joy for Jewish mothers because these celebrations involve all our favorite things: family, food; family, fun; family, frivolity. (Did I mention family?)

For a Jewish mother, the holidays mean happiness, family, and fun. They also mean a lot of work. In this chapter, you'll explore our role in traditional Jewish celebrations.

The Jewish Holidays in Brief

The following chart focuses on that quintessential Jewish obsession: food. The chart provides a handy-dandy overview of the holidays. This will prove especially useful for those of you Jewish mothers raised in very secular homes. For those of you already exhausted by preparing for the holidays, use the chart to decide when to put the pressure on your sister-in-law to host the festivities.

Diet Guide to the Jewish Holidays

Jewish Holiday	What to Do
Rosh Hashanah	Feast
Tzom Gedalia	Fast
Yom Kippur	More fasting
Succoth	Feast
Simchat Torah	Keep feasting
Hanukkah	Eat potato pancakes
Tenth of Tevet	Do not eat potato pancakes

Tu B'Shevat	Feast
Purim	Eat pastry
Passover	Do not eat pastry
Shavuot	Dairy feast (cheesecake, blintzes, etc.)

Now, let's turn to the High Holy Days: Rosh Hashanah and Yom Kippur. The holiest holidays in the Jewish calendar, these holidays celebrate judgment and forgiveness. These are the biggies, ladies and gentlemen.

Rosh Hashanah

Rosh Hashanah (rawsh ha-SHAW-neh), the Jewish New Year, celebrates the day that the world was created. It starts the atonement period that ends ten days later with Yom Kippur. Orthodox Jews believe that on Rosh Hashanah, all Jews stand before God for judgment. (The Lord makes His decision on the last of the ten days, Yom Kippur.)

Rosh Hashanah extends over the first two days of the Hebrew month of Tishrei, which usually corresponds to September. Orthodox and Conservative Jews celebrate for two days; Reform Jews, for one day. As with all Jewish holidays, the date of Rosh Hashanah is determined by the Jewish lunar calendar. The following chart shows when Rosh Hashanah falls for three sample years.

Jewish Calendar	American Calendar
5768	9/12/2007
5769	9/29/2008
5770	9/19/2009

The Jewish New Year isn't the noise-making, drunken revelry that has come to characterize the American New Year. Dick Clark isn't invited to the party; we don't freeze our tuchus off in Times Square. Instead, Rosh Hashanah is a solemn and a joyous time. We repent, but we also gather with family and friends to feast and eat sweet things, especially apples and honey to symbolize a sweet new year. What do Jewish mothers do on the Jewish New Year? They cook and clean. They serve and socialize. In short, they run the show.

Happy New Year!

The traditional greeting on Rosh Hashanah is *Leshana tova*, Hebrew for "A good year."

Yom Kippur

Yom Kippur (yum KIP-per) is the Day of Atonement. On this day, the holiest and most solemn of all Jewish holidays, we fast.

This means no food or drink at all. The holiday's central theme is atonement and reconciliation. The Yom Kippur services begin with a prayer known as Kol Nidrei, recited before sunset.

Observant Jews also do the following:

* Spend the day in the synagogue.
* Ask those we have offended for forgiveness.
* Pray and look inward.

Here's your shorthand: Think of Yom Yippur as instant Lent. Now for two joyous holidays: Hanukkah and Purim.

Hanukkah

Hanukkah (KHON-eh-keh), also known as the Festival of Lights, is an eight-day Jewish holiday that starts on the twenty-fifth day of Kislev in the Hebrew calendar. Since Hanukkah falls in December, some non-Jews have typecast it as the Jewish Christmas. It's not. It's also not a major Jewish holiday. It's a minor Jewish holiday, even though Wal-Mart sells Hanukkah lights. Nonetheless, in the spirit of Keeping Up with the Goyim, some Jewish families make Hanukkah a Jewish alternative to Christmas. From a kid's standpoint, this does have some advantages. What do Jewish mothers do during Hanukkah? They cook and clean. They serve and socialize. In short, they run the show. Are we seeing a pattern here?

The Story of Hanukkah

This is one of those holidays that falls into the category of "They tried to kill us but we won, so let's eat." Hanukkah commemorates the victory of the Jewish Maccabees over the Syrian tyrants in 167 B.C.E in a fight for religious freedom. The story goes this way: Judah the Maccabee and his father Mattathias led three years of guerrilla warfare against Antiochus IV, who had the foolish idea of converting the Jews to the Greek religion. To that end, Antiochus ordered the Jews to stop circumcising their infant sons, build shrines to the Greek gods, and so on. The Jewish cause seemed hopeless because the Syrians had all the firepower. It seemed especially bleak when the Syrians sacked and burned the Temple.

Soon after, the Jews returned to Jerusalem to the destroyed Temple and set about restoring it. In 165 B.C.E., Judah the Maccabee rededicated the Temple by lighting a great candelabra called a *menorah*.

There was only enough oil to light the menorah for one day. Miraculously, the oil burned for eight days—which was the length of time it took to press, prepare, and consecrate new oil.

This delightful holiday is often celebrated with:

* Parties, games, and small gifts to children; money and chocolate "coins" are popular.
* Oily foods, especially potato pancakes (*latkes*) and doughnuts.
* A game with a top called a dreidel.

Top Reasons to Like Hanukkah

* Annoying your mother as you play with the wax that drips from the menorah.
* Avoiding roof damage from reindeer.
* Using your fireplace without fear of hurting a jolly fat man in a red suit.
* Shunning Irving Berlin holiday songs.
* Stuffing your face with latkes.

And the number one reason to like Hanukkah: playing with family and friends.

Purim

Purim (pronounced POOR-im) commemorates the rescue of the Jews of Persia from Haman's plot to kill them all. Who saved the day? A Jewish mother, the beautiful Queen Esther. Purim is often celebrated by:

* Reading the Book of Esther in synagogue. When Haman's name is said, kids boo and make a racket with noisemakers. This is not a good holiday for those afflicted with migraines.
* Giving food and money to the poor.
* Exchanging gifts and food with family and friends. Our family friend Matt Seigelman always sends me a charming package with cool stuff like granola bars and raisins. Since he's usually halfway around the world at the time doing business in India, his thoughtfulness is especially appreciated.
* Holding great carnival-like events and parties.
* Wearing masks and costumes.

Hamantashen, three-cornered filled cookies, are often served during Purim. See Chapter 17 for a description of these yummy pastries.

What do Jewish mothers do on Purim? They cook and clean. They serve and socialize. In short, they run the show. Catch the pattern?

Passover

Passover (called Pesach in Yiddish) is the Jewish festival of freedom. In America, it's celebrated for eight days; in Israel, for seven days. As with Hannukah and Purim, Passover celebrates our deliverance. In this case, it's our freedom from enslavement in Egypt more than 3,200 years ago. As described in the Book of Exodus, Passover marks the "birth" of the Jewish nation, as the Jews' ancestors were freed from being Pharaoh's slaves and allowed to become servants of God instead.

The word *Passover* comes from Moses' words that God "will pass over" the houses of the Israelites during the final plague of the Ten Plagues of Egypt, the killing of the first-born. On the night of that plague, the Israelites sacrificed the paschal lamb, smeared their lintels and doorposts with the lamb's blood, and ate the roasted sacrifice in a celebratory feast.

Passover begins on the 15th day of Nisan on the Hebrew calendar, which falls between March 15 and April 30 on the American calendar. What do Jewish mothers do on Passover? They cook and clean. They serve and socialize. In short, they run the show. Can't miss that pattern, can you, ladies?

The Story of Passover

The Pharaoh ordered all male Jewish babies be killed. One couple—Jochebed and her husband Amram—tried to save their baby. Jochebed hid the baby for three months. Finally, when it became apparent that the infant was going to be discovered and killed, she placed him in a tiny boat. This she sent down the Nile River, hoping that he would somehow be saved. Her prayers were answered: Pharaoh's daughter rescued the baby, named him Moses, and raised him as her own son. When he grew up, Moses learned that he was Jewish and tried to convince the Pharaoh to free the Jewish people, but guess what: Pharaoh refused.

God sent ten plagues down on Egypt, but still the Pharaoh wouldn't let the Jews go. For the next time you play Trivial Pursuit or appear on *Jeopardy!*, the Ten Plagues are:

1. Rivers and other water sources turned to blood (Exodus 7:14–25)
2. Reptiles, commonly believed to be frogs (Exodus 7:26–8:11)
3. Lice (Exodus 8:12–15)
4. Flies, wild animals, or beetles (Exodus 8:16–28)
5. Disease on livestock (Exodus 9:1–7)
6. Boils (Exodus 9:8–12)
7. Hail and fire (Exodus 9:13–35)
8. Locusts (Exodus 10:1–20)
9. Darkness (Exodus 10:21–29)
10. Death of the firstborn (Exodus 11:1–12:36)

Let's focus on that tenth and final plague—the death of all Egyptian first-born males. No one escaped, from the first-born of livestock to the lowest servant to Pharaoh's own first-born son. In the middle of the night, God Himself came upon Egypt and directed the Angel of Death to take the life of all the Egyptian first-born sons, including Pharaoh's son. That night, there was a great cry in Egypt, such as had never been heard before, or ever will be heard again. However, no Hebrew first-born was killed, as God "passed over" the Israelite houses.

After this, Pharaoh ordered the Israelites to leave Egypt. The Israelites didn't hesitate, and at the end of that night Moses led them out of Egypt. They gathered up their belongings so quickly that they didn't have time for their bread to rise. They baked it fast and took it the way it was—flat.

But Pharaoh changed his mind and sent his army after the Jews to bring them back. God parted the Red Sea for the Jews to cross, and as soon as they were safely on the other side, the waters closed on the soldiers, drowning them all.

The Seder

On Passover, we retell the story of our liberation in a ritual meal called a Seder (SAY-der). The word *Seder* means "order," and we read the Passover story in a special order from the book

The Portable Jewish Mother

called a Haggadah. The Seder plate contains various symbolic foods that will be eaten or referred to during the course of the meal. The Seder helps us pass on the traditions of Judaism from one generation to another.

The Seder Plate

The six foods served during the Seder are arranged on a special Seder plate. Each of the foods is used during the ritual meal to help retell the story of the Jews' Exodus from slavery in Egypt.

The food arrayed on the Seder plate and used during the Passover Seder is highly symbolic. All the food together stands for slavery and freedom; each food also has a specific meaning. The first half of the Seder commemorates slavery; the second half, freedom. Thus, the matzoh, bitter herbs, and charoset served during the first half all symbolize the slavery of the Jewish people. The charoset individually symbolizes the mortar that the Jewish slaves used as they cemented bricks. During the second half of the Seder, the matzoh and wine celebrate our delivery from slavery. During this part of the Seder, the matzoh now represents the bread of freedom.

The Four Questions

As part of the Seder, four questions are asked. Usually, the youngest child gets the honor. The most famous question is "Why is this night different from all other nights?" To a kid, this is always a high point in the ceremony.

Housecleaning

As part of the preparation for Passover, observant Jewish women remove leavened products from the home. Clearly, a Jewish mother's work is never done. This manic housecleaning commemorates the fact that the Jews left Egypt in such a hurry that they didn't have time to let their bread rise. It is also a symbolic way of removing the "puffiness" (arrogance, pride) from our souls.

Anything made from the five major grains—wheat, rye, oats, barley, and splet—that hasn't been cooked within 18 minutes after being in water is forbidden. These leavened products are called *chametz*. Instead of eating leavened carbs during Passover, we eat matzohs, the flat, unleavened "bread" that recalls the hurriedly-baked bread that the Israelites ate after their hasty departure from Egypt. I happen to love the taste of matzoh, but some people think it tastes like paper. How often they've chewed paper, I don't know.

The Party's Over

When Jews go to meet their maker, it's traditional for the burial to take place as soon as possible, even on the same day of the death, but no more than two nights after the death. Only plain wooden coffins are used in Jewish funerals because Jews believe that we don't preserve the body because Jews don't believe that the body should be preserved. Why? As the body decays, the soul ascends to Heaven.

Shiva

The mourning period, called *shiva* (SHI-vah), begins with the funeral. Traditionally, it lasts seven solemn days. Here's what mourning members of the immediate family do in observant Jewish homes:

* Stay home and don't work.
* Wear cloth slippers.
* Sit on stools or the floor.
* Refrain from sex.
* Refrain from shaving, bathing, or anything associated with vanity.
* Wear clothing with a rip in the lapel (today, this is usually observed with a small piece of black fabric pinned on the lapel).

Friends come to visit during the shiva and offer sympathy and comfort.

Jewish Law and Cremation

Judaism has traditionally disapproved of cremation. However, during the 1800s, many Jewish cemeteries in Europe filled up. To deal with this real estate shortage, Liberal Jews began to accept cremation instead of burial. Nonetheless, Orthodox Jews still oppose cremation, believing the soul of a cremated person will become a restless wanderer for eternity. Many Orthodox Jews also shun cremation because of the horrific overtones of the Holocaust, when the bodies of millions of murdered Jews were destroyed in fire pits.

A Silly Shiva Joke

A Native American comes back to the reservation to visit his parents after spending some time in New York (that den of sin and iniquity). He announces to his father, "I've fallen in love with a nice Jewish girl."

His father, horrified, replied, "You're betraying your heritage. It will break your mother's heart that you're not marrying a nice Native American girl. Jews feel the same way and you'll be ostracized in both camps."

The son reassures his father: "Don't worry. They must have already accepted the situation because they have already given their daughter a Native American name."

"Really?" says the father. "What name?"

The son answers, "Sitting Shiva."

In the next chapter, you'll learn how to have some fun when you stop cooking and cleaning and running the show!

Jewish Soul Food

Part 1: Appetizers

Italians have their lasagna, the Irish their corned beef, the Germans their sausages . . . and the Jews? We have it all! In this chapter, learn how to cook some appetizers to get the party started.

A prominent and respected Jewish businessman died, and the community gathered in the synagogue to honor him. The rabbi intoned solemnly, "Our dear departed Saul will be sorely missed. He was a good husband, a loving father, he was. . . ." At this point a tiny old lady at the back shouts, "Give him some chicken soup!"

The rabbi discreetly ignores her and goes on, "Saul was a beloved community man, a pillar of the synagogue, a fine businessman. . . ."

And the old lady shouts louder, "Give him some chicken soup!"

The rabbi can't ignore her any longer, so he responds, "Dear lady, our brother is departed; chicken soup can't help him now."

The lady shouts back, "So—it couldn't hurt him."

From a Jewish mother's standpoint, she's perfectly correct. There's not a lot that can't be fixed by a good bowl of chicken soup (also known as "Jewish penicillin"). So, Jewish mothers, see how your recipe for this miracle cure compares to the one that I've got for you in this chapter.

Jewish holidays reinforce the importance of eating because we celebrate with food, console with food, and compensate with food. Fortunately, when it comes to food, Jewish mothers consider every day a holiday. That's because we show love with food.

Thus, we can conclude that to be a good Jewish mother, you have to know how to do food. Not to worry, bubbulah; being a superb Jewish cook is easy: Just heap a lot of top-quality fresh food on the table, step back, and let them dive in. In this chapter, I'll give you some guidelines for serving yummy Jewish-style foods—especially chicken soup!

Instant Yiddish

Bubbulah is a Yiddish term that means "darling." Don't confuse it with *bubblah*, which is a New England term for what otherwise well-spoken people call a water fountain. This term is especially common in Rhode Island and Massachusetts. These flinty folks consider those who use the term "water fountain" to be putting on airs.

The Primacy of Food and Feeding to a Jewish Mother

When it comes to what matters to a Jewish mother and what defines a Jewish mother, we're in a dead heat between the intangibles—guilt, worry, education, and advocacy—and the tangibles: children, grandchildren, and food. Now, I can't do anything about assisting you in the bedroom (nor do I want to), but I'm a regular Jewish Martha Stewart when it comes to setting a table—without the fraud conviction, blond hair, and Connecticut estate. To a Jewish mother, food offers an opportunity to give great comfort, a hug in a bowl. My friend Professor Barbara Bengels shared this food memory: "My very Jewish grandmother from Romania was a factor only in my very early years. All I remember about her was her 'luchen' (noodle) soup with chicken feet, and the words 'Eat up,' maybe the only English she knew. My mother told me when I was an adult that the size of the bowls of soup I was given as a four-year-old were enough to feed a whole army."

Food is so very important to being a Jewish mother that it deserves more than one chapter. It deserves an entire book, in fact, but I don't want to make you zaftig (plump). So I'll treat you to two chapters only. Be aware, however, that to a Jewish mother, food has the potential to solve all ills: the nuclear crisis in Korea, the devaluation of the dollar against the euro, and your child's skinned knee.

. . . .

Instant Yiddish

Zaftig is a Yiddish word that literally means "juicy." Pronounced ZOFF-tig, it conveys a delightful abundance of flesh, a Rubenesque surfeit of femininity.

. . . .

Food Primer, Jewish-Style

To a traditional Jewish grandmother, all food not homemade by your own two hands is by definition dirty. Ice cream from the truck is filthy and will surely give you cooties. Food from a friend's lunchbox is suspect: After all, who knows if those are really top-quality cold cuts? Meat on a stick from a sidewalk vendor? Put a knife through your mother's heart right away. Even fresh fruit from a sidewalk kiosk is suspect. We all know those strawberries are covered in road grit.

But modern Jewish mothers are an accomplished and sensible lot and realize that some relaxation of the rules is necessary. This is especially true today when even more women are working while schlepping their kids to Diaper Dippers and Gymboree. This is why we have takeout. Repeat after me: There is nothing wrong with a nice takeout chicken from your local supermarket or Costco. If you're feeling a bit inadequate, get a dozen chickens (one for each person and a few extra for a nosh at midnight), toss some rosemary on top for that gourmet touch, and lie about it. "So what if I toiled all day as a systems analyst on Wall Street?" you declaim brightly. "I came home a bit early to put in the chickens. How can I have my family eat take-out?" Just be sure to hide the telltale takeout bags.

Spring Happy Surprise Takeout—or, Hungry Again in Fifteen Minutes

Chinese food is also a fine substitute for a homemade meal. Keep the menu on the fridge for quick reference. Put the telephone number of your favorite take-out restaurant on speed dial at home and on your cell. Memorize the item numbers to save even more time. That way, you can just push one button and say, "I need a #2, a large #14, and two #28s. Sauce on the side. Hold the MSG. Add extra almond cookies. Thanks!"

Cheeses of Nazareth

In a pinch, deli always works: a few tubs of tuna salad, a container of egg salad, a loaf of rye, and you're all set. Throw some celery and carrot sticks on the table for color. Whitefish, lox, and cream cheese are the upscale version of this quick meal, but in my experience, this treat is reserved for brunch, not dinner.

Kosher Food

So what's kosher? Food that is kahrut or kahruth (translated as "kosher" in English) is fit for consumption by observant Jews. Non-kosher food is called treifah or tareif, which translates as "tref." Here's the very least you need to know:

* Food derived from animals must be from kosher animals as listed in the Bible. Pork, shellfish, and certain other meat products are never kosher.
* Meat products from kosher animals must be slaughtered in a specific manner.
* Don't mix dairy and meat. Further, you must use separate utensils for meat and milk food preparation, consumption, and storage.
* Certain agricultural products are restricted, such as fruits of a tree that is in its first three years, and produce of Israel that has not been tithed.
* Leavened bread and products are not kosher during Passover (a holiday that occurs in the spring).

The kosher rules are not that simple, of course, which means that unless you keep a kosher kitchen, you can't just whip up a kosher meal. Kosher food and Jewish food are *not* the same. Kosher food has been slaughtered, harvested, and prepared according to the specific laws you just read. As you'll learn later in this chapter, Jewish food is a unique blend of foods from around the world that fulfill the kosher laws and/or taste good.

Different sources give different reasons for the kosher laws. Some argue that the laws were designed thousands of years ago to prevent people from eating unhealthy foods. Shellfish, for instance, can go south long before it gets stinky. Other sources say the dietary laws had nothing to do with health: Rather, the dietary laws were a way for Jews to set themselves off from non-Jews. This theory has Biblical backing: According to the Book of Leviticus, the kosher laws are linked to ritual purity and holiness. Still other Jewish biblical scholars believe that the kosher laws were designed to make Jews think and ponder. The food laws thus are just another kick in the pants to remind us that the universe may be generally rational, but humankind cannot possibly understand everything.

In general, Orthodox and Conservative Judaism believes that observant Jews should follow the laws of kahrut. Some Reform and Deconstructionist Jews don't believe the laws are relevant anymore. Many Jews who don't follow the laws strictly nonetheless avoid drinking milk with a hamburger and shun pork roasts, even when glazed with bourbon and orange marmalade.

Now that you know the basics, let's get into the real Jewish eating.

Instant Kosher

Vegetarians and vegans are in effect following the laws of kahrut—as long as the milk, wine, and bread are supervised and the utensils were only used for kosher food (never used for unsupervised milk).

Some Traditional Jewish Foods to Know and Love

All cultures have foods that are immediately linked with them. The Poles have their pierogi; the French, their fries. People in Maryland chow down on crabs; Bostoners get gassy as a result of their baked beans. Jewish cuisine is very different from all of these, however; because of the Jewish Diaspora, Jewish cooking is a compilation of many different foods.

Jewish dishes are in many ways the same as local dishes. For instance, Ashkenazi Jews eat the hearty (some say leaden) foods that come from their ancestral homes in central and eastern Europe. Thus, a traditional Sabbath meal for Ashkenazi Jews would likely be a rich beef brisket in gravy, a savory potato or sweet noodle pudding, and challah bread. Sephardic Jews, in contrast, eat lighter foods that are common in their Mediterranean homelands. A traditional Sabbath meal for Sephardic Jews would likely be a meat dish; a tomato, hummus, and avocado salad; stuffed grape leaves; and rice.

Nonetheless, when we think of "Jewish foods," certain dishes come to mind. Below are some of the ones you're likely to encounter and perhaps even want to prepare. I've included recipes for my personal favorites. I make no claim to impartiality or observance of kosher laws. The following list and recipes merely reflect what I like to cook and eat. And since family and friends always leave *my* table happy (and keep coming back for years), you shouldn't complain.

The Portable Jewish Mother

Appetizers

To make your life easier, I've added notes on each dish. Remember that I'm being highly idiosyncratic rather than authoritative or observant.

Start with a Little Nosh

Food	Description
baba ghanouj	A lovely eggplant spread.
blintzes	Delicate crepes that are stuffed with cheese or fruits and then fried in butter. Lovely, lovely, lovely!
borscht	A beautiful clear red beet soup, usually served cold with a dollop of sour cream. I think it's both attractive and delicious but non–borscht aficionados rarely share my enthusiasm for beets in general, much less as a soup.
burekas	Filled dough pockets that are widely sold on Israeli street corners.
chicken soup	This classic dish also makes a great main course.
chopped liver	Chicken livers are cooked and mixed with fat and onions. Not for the faint of heart or those who want their heart to remain functional.

gefilte fish	You won't find a "gefilte fish" swimming around the tank at the fishmongers: This delicate fish patty is made of different ground-up fish, usually carp, pike, and whitefish. It contains carrots, onions, and spices as well.
herring	Sold in jars, the herring comes marinated in a sour cream sauce.
knishes	In the most traditional versions, these pastry squares are filled with mashed potatoes, ground meat, sauerkraut, onions, kasha (buckwheat groats), or cheese. Modern fillings include sweet potatoes, black beans, fruit, broccoli, tofu, or spinach. Fey on the modern varieties: Purists rank them right up there with the abomination called pineapple pizza.
tabouli	This Middle Eastern dish is a combination of bulgur, parsley, mint, tomato, and scallions, chopped with lemon juice and various seasonings, generally including black pepper and sometimes cinnamon and allspice.
whitefish salad	You gotta like fish. I don't.

The Portable Jewish Mother

Classic Jewish Chicken Soup

Chicken soup, also known as "Jewish penicillin," is easy to make and I've never found anyone who doesn't like a steaming hot bowl of chicken soup. It freezes very well, too, so you can always have it on hand when someone comes down with the sniffles. By serving variations on the basic soup, you can fool your family into thinking they're having lots of different meals: one night add matzoh balls; another night, throw in a handful of egg noodles; a third night, some rice. Perhaps best of all, chicken soup is a very forgiving recipe. Add a little too much of this or that and it doesn't matter at all. No one will notice or care. (If they do kvetch, smack them with the soup ladle and tell them they should only starve.)

All Jewish cooks have their own chicken soup recipe, so don't be e-mailing me to complain that I left out the dill or what's with the bouillon cubes. That said, here's a basic fool-proof recipe for Jewish chicken soup.

Ingredients

1	chicken, cut up (a fowl, an older bird, works best because it has the most flavor)
2	onions, diced
3	stalks of celery, diced
3	carrots, diced
3–5	chicken bouillon cubes
	Handful of parsley
	Salt, pepper
5	cups cold water

Method

1. You'll need a large soup pot. Put everything in the pot but the water. Add the water last. (This way, you don't end up splashing water all over the kitchen when you plop the chicken in.) Cover the pot with a tight-fitting lid.
2. Bring the soup to a boil. Reduce heat and simmer for one hour to an hour and a half.
3. Take the chicken out of the pot. Remove the chicken from the bone and chop into bite-size pieces. This is easier if the chicken is cool, but not as much fun.
4. Cool soup in the refrigerator until completely cold. Remove congealed fat. Serve the fat as schmaltz (like

butter on bread) to someone you want to kill. You can also use it to fry onions. It's delicious but deadly. Otherwise, throw the fat out.

5. At this point, some people strain the soup and throw away the veggies. I don't because why waste good food? Leave in all those nice mushy veggies and add some of the chicken you cut up.

6. Heat the soup. Add noodles, rice, or matzoh balls. Season to taste. (If you're having a very bad, awful day, add noodles, rice, *and* matzoh balls, pop in your DVD of *Fiddler on the Roof*, and slurp down the soup. A good starch overload always makes you feel better fast.)

7. Enjoy!

Light, Fluffy Matzoh Balls

Some people like their matzoh balls as lead sinkers, heavy and chewy. These matzoh balls are Oh! so tasty going down, but they sit in your stomach for days like rocks. Other people like their matzoh balls light and fluffy, little bits of heaven. Fortunately, there's an easy way to make everyone happy: Serve the matzoh balls immediately and they'll be light. Let them sit a while and they'll crash land. Following is my recipe.

Ingredients

4	large eggs
½	cup club soda (This is the secret ingredient for fluffy matzoh balls. Use broth or water and they'll be heavier.)
3	tablespoons corn oil or chicken fat. (And a little extra for your hands, later.)
2	cups matzoh meal
	Salt to taste

Method

1. Using a fork, blend eggs. Add other ingredients.
2. Cover and refrigerate the batter for about an hour. The batter is pretty indestructible, so you can make the matzoh balls hours later if you get distracted, as I always do.
3. Rub some oil on your hands. Form balls. They're usually about 2 tablespoons per ball, but you can make them any size you like—just cook larger ones longer and smaller ones for less time. Each cup of matzoh meal makes about 12 balls in the 2-tablespoon size.
4. Boil in water or soup for 25–34 minutes. Keep the pot covered and don't peek!
5. Serve the matzoh balls in soup or just pick them out with a slotted spoon and snake them down over the pot. You'll pay later, but it's so worth it.

Matzoh Balls and Basic Chemistry

Be sure to use a big pot when you simmer the matzoh balls. Matzoh balls expand to twice their original size while simmering.

In Chapter 16, you'll learn all about the main courses that Jewish mothers have made for years. And like a well-made matzoh ball, many of these dishes really stick to your ribs . . . and your hips.

Jewish Soul Food

Part 2: Main Courses

Two Chinese men are leaving
Bloom's restaurant and one says to the
other, "The problem with Jewish food is that
two days later, you're hungry again."

Not with the main courses in this chapter. They'll
hold you for a good week. And then some.

Main Courses

Below are some of my favorite Jewish mother main course dishes. They're what I consider "Jewish-style," which means that they're traditional in Jewish culture but not kosher.

The Main Event

Food	Description
baked or roasted chicken	Can't go wrong.
boiled tongue	Exactly what the name says. Fortunately, it tastes better than it sounds.
brisket	This is pot roast with a fancy name. A classic European Jewish dish, it tastes even better reheated the second day.
corned beef	Not served with cabbage.
fish	Whatever type of fish that floats your boat, as long as it has fins.
Hebrew National hot dogs	My friend-who's-like-a-brother Stephan Gary Kravitz insists I include Hebrew National hot dogs as a main dish. Who am I to argue?
kasha	This buckwheat groats dish is at least 1,000 years old.

kishkes	*Kishke* is the Yiddish word for intestines, as in, "Ach! Such a pain I have in my kishkes." Traditionally, this dish was made by stuffing the intestines of a cow with a meat or bread filling. Today, you can buy prepared kishkes in a plastic tubing. It shows up at traditional Jewish weddings and bar/bat mitzvahs and is far tastier than the name suggests.
kugel	This pudding-like dish is made with noodles or potatoes. It can be sweet or savory. I eat it as a main course because I like it so much, but it's more traditionally served as a side dish.
latkes	Traditionally, these fried pancakes are made with potatoes and onions, but they can also be made with matzoh meal. The packaged matzoh meal mix isn't half bad, in a pinch.
matzoh brie	Soaked matzohs are added to eggs and then the whole mess is fried. I love it, but my husband thinks it tastes like wallpaper paste. Who knows when he last ate wallpaper paste?
stuffed cabbage	There are many different variations, but my favorite involves cabbage leaves stuffed with beef and rice and cooked in tomato sauce. I throw in some ginger snaps as well.

The Portable Jewish Mother

Potato Latkes

Potato latkes are traditionally served during Hanukkah, the Jewish Festival of Lights. That's because oil plays a key symbolic role in many foods served during the holiday. Latkes are usually accompanied by applesauce and sour cream. Unfortunately, latkes are a nuisance to make and don't keep well, so the cook (that's you, kiddo) ends up spending hours slaving over a hot frying pan. But there are those people, especially my son, who swear that a good latke is worth all the effort it entails. Naturally, that's because his Jewish mother is doing the cooking!

Ingredients

2	medium potatoes
1	onion
1	egg
¼	cup flour or matzoh meal
	Salt and pepper to taste
	Lots of vegetable oil for frying

Method

1. Peel and coarsely grate the potatoes; set aside. Peel and coarsely grate the onion. I STRONGLY suggest that you use a food processor for this or you'll be at it for hours.
2. Using your hands, squeeze out all the potato water.
3. Mix the grated onions and potatoes with the beaten egg, flour or matzoh meal, salt, and pepper.
4. Fill a frying pan with at least two inches of oil. Heat the oil until it's hot enough to fry food crisply.
5. Drop teaspoon-size pancakes into hot vegetable oil. Flatten with the spatula.
6. Fry until brown on both sides.

The recipe doubles and quadruples perfectly. If you've never made latkes before, you'll be shocked at how many everyone can eat, so be sure to make a lot more than you think you'll need. Trust me: You'll need them.

The Staff of Life

Traditional Jewish breads are challah, rye, pumpernickel, bagels, and pita. Challah, however, is the essential part of any Jewish meal. This light egg bread makes a superb French toast the day after the meal. A challah is long and oval with a braided top.

Noodle Kugel

As you read earlier, kugels come in potato and noodle varieties, savory and sweet. Traditional Jewish mothers are divided on this issue: You have your sweet kugel camp and your savory kugel camp. My family loves the sweet noodle kugel I make, which has become a Thanksgiving staple in my house. It's easy to make and delicious. (Bet you figured out what side of this issue I'm on!)

Ingredients

5	eggs
½	cup sugar
1	8-ounce container sour cream
8	ounces cream cheese (one bar, or a tub of whipped cream cheese)
1	pound wide egg noodles, cooked and drained
	Salt to taste

Method

1. Separate the eggs. Whip the egg whites until stiff. For best results, use a glass or metal bowl rather than a plastic one.
2. In another bowl, mix egg yolks, sugar, sour cream, and cream cheese until smooth. Use a hand mixer or your arm will ache.

3. Fold in cooked noodles.
4. Fold in whipped egg whites.
5. Spoon into greased 13" × 9" pan. Bake about 50 minutes at 350°. The kugel should be lightly browned but not dry.

If you're like me and count calories, you can use low-fat or non-fat sour cream and cream cheese. If you're not like me and don't know from calories, you can spread a can of cherry pie filling on top of the cooked kugel. Some people also add a layer of corn-flake crumbs before baking. Then you have your raisin fans. . . . Jewish foods are very flexible and forgiving, as you can see. Who ever heard of raisins in a lasagna?

Beef Brisket, Jewish Style

Butchers traditionally prepare two different cuts of brisket: a flat cut and a point cut. Both cuts are boneless. In addition, they both come from the same part of the cow — the foreshank and the breast. The difference between them is in the amount of fat on each cut. The flat cut is less fatty and thus more expensive. Whether the flat cut or the point cut, brisket is a tough meat and needs to be cooked a long time. Since it has a high fat content, however, it's quite tasty.

Jewish mothers who aren't purists on the issue of the cut of meat will use any large cut of beef, such as a top or bottom roast, as well as a brisket. I love slow-cooked beef in a rich sauce, so I'm happy with just about any cut of beef. And I'm not fussy about the name: Call it a pot roast, brisket, or whatever you want. Just give me seconds.

There are literally hundreds of ways to make brisket. Some Jewish mothers mix a few packages of dried onion soup mix with water, seal the brisket in foil, and bake it. Other Jewish mothers pour in a bottle of catsup. Still others use dry onion soup mix, ketchup, and a bottle of ginger ale. Other brisket ingredients include brown sugar, vinegar, Worcestershire sauce, coffee, prepared barbecue sauce, Coca-Cola, honey, and red wine. Like so many other Jewish foods, brisket is an easy, inexpensive, and forgiving dish. Below is a classic recipe from a classic Jewish mother I know. Feel free to experiment to your heart's desire. It's indestructible.

I always prepare the meat a day ahead, cool it overnight, and remove all the fat. Then I reheat it and serve.

Ingredients

	Several cloves of garlic, peeled and diced
6–8	pounds beef brisket
	Salt and pepper
½	cup flour
1	pound carrots, peeled and sliced
3	large onions, peeled and chopped
2–3	pounds white potatoes, peeled and cut into large chunks
5–6	bay leaves

Method

1. Rub the garlic into the beef.
2. Put the salt, pepper, and flour in a plastic bag or on a piece of waxed paper. Coat the meat with the mixture.
3. Place all the vegetables in the bottom of a large ovenproof pan. Traditional cooks use a cast-iron Dutch oven, but these women all look like Hulk Hogan. Add the bay leaves.
4. Place the brisket on top of the vegetables.
5. Add water to cover the vegetables.
6. Bake at 325° about 45 minutes per pound. To test for doneness, stick a fork in the meat. It should be very tender.

The Portable Jewish Mother

CHAPTER 17

Jewish Soul Food

Part 3: Desserts

I could easily pass the appetizers and main courses and go straight to dessert. That's not only because I have a sweet tooth but also because I think a Jewish Mother's desserts are simply superb. Here are my favorites.

End with Something Sweet

Food	Description
apple strudel	So nice with a scoop of vanilla ice cream.
bobke	This light, yeasty cake often has ribbons of nuts, chocolate, or cheese running through it. I know I'll get letters of complaint, but I'm a serious cook and in my long years of experience, the bakery bobke is better than anything I can make at home.
cheesecake	Recipe follows, since a Jewish mother's cheesecake is a primal food, and rightfully so.
halvah	I adore this heavenly sesame seed candy, but my daughter thinks it tastes like sand. The most common varieties are vanilla, chocolate, and pistachio. Halvah is rich, so a little goes a long way on your hips and tuchus.
hamantashen (a.k.a. hamantaschen, homentashen)	These jam-filled sugar cookies, traditionally eaten during the holiday of Purim, have three corners. They are shaped like the hat of Haman the tyrant; hence their name.
honey cake	A traditional Passover treat.
jelly doughnuts	See honey cake.

The Portable Jewish Mother

macaroons	Coconut cookies, sometimes dipped in chocolate, which is like gilding the lily.
mandelbrodt	Like a pound cake, studded with walnuts, candied fruits, and chocolate. It's usually served in small slices.
rugelach	My great good friend (and Jewish mother) Jodi Saviuk makes the world's best rugelach, a cream cheese–based cookie filled with nuts and raisins. They're far too much work for me to make and besides, no one makes them as yummy as Jodi does.
sponge cake	This light, golden cake is a snap to prepare and a real crowd-pleaser.

Sponge Cake

I've had this recipe for thirty years, so there's no way I can trace its origin. It's fast, easy, and very forgiving—even novice Jewish mothers can turn out a spectacular cake. I apologize in advance to whomever gave this recipe to me. Send me an e-mail and I'll give you credit in the second edition of this book.

Ingredients

3–6	eggs
1	cup sugar
¼	cup boiling water
1	teaspoon vanilla or almond flavoring
1	teaspoon lemon or orange rind, optional
1	cup flour
1½	teaspoons baking powder
¾	teaspoon salt

Method

1. Separate the eggs. Beat the whites until stiff.
2. In another bowl, beat the egg yolks until pale yellow. This will take about 5 minutes with an electric beater.
3. Add the sugar to the egg yolks gradually.
4. Slowly add the boiling water. Don't burn yourself!
5. Add all the other ingredients but the egg whites.
6. Fold in the egg whites.
7. Pour the batter in an UNGREASED tube pan, the kind that comes in two parts. It has a removable outer ring.
8. Bake at 350° about 45 minutes, until the tester (toothpick) comes out dry.

This cake is delicious plain but also scrumptious with ice cream, sherbet, and whipped cream. It's especially great after a heavy meal because it's so light.

Lenore Strober's Cheesecake

Cheesecake is one of the most common desserts in the world and perhaps one of the oldest involving dairy other than milk. Jewish cheesecakes (also called "New York style" cheesecakes) are made with cream cheese, eggs, and often heavy cream or sour cream. Lindy's and Junior's Deli helped make this luscious dessert popular.

My dear friend Lenore Strober, a Jewish mother five times over (as well as surrogate Jewish mother to many of her colleagues at Commack High School South), was one of the finest cooks and hostesses I ever met. She was famous for the spectacular table she set but even more for her warmth and love. Her Jewish mother cheesecake is simply the best. She'd be delighted that I'm passing on the goodness.

Ingredients

	Butter (for greasing pan)
1	cup graham cracker crumbs
2	teaspoons cinnamon
4	eggs
4	bars of cream cheese (NOT whipped); must be at room temperature
1	cup sugar
1	cup sour cream
1	teaspoon vanilla
2	tablespoons flour

Method

1. Heavily grease 8" or 9" springform pan with butter. Mix graham cracker crumbs and cinnamon. Spread in the pan and shake the pan so the bottom and sides get coated.
2. Separate the eggs. In a medium bowl, beat the whites until stiff.
3. In a large bowl, combine the egg yolks with all the other ingredients except egg whites. Blend until smooth.
4. Fold egg whites into mixture.
5. Pour into pan. Bake at 275° for 1½ hours. Turn off oven. Leave the cake in the oven another hour.

The Portable Jewish Mother

6. Garnish with fresh fruit (strawberries or blueberries are delicious), canned pie filling, or a sprinkling of powdered sugar.

Cheesecake Savvy

Bake your cheesecake in a water bath to prevent cracks. Easiest way: Set the springform pan in another pan of water. If this makes you nervous, put a separate pan of water next to the cheesecake.

Also, be sure to chill your cheesecake completely before slicing or it will crumble.

An Important Note on Bagels

Jewish mothers know the culinary and emotional value of a bagel. Bagels can be served morning, noon, and night. They're fine toasted or not. They keep well, assuming your family doesn't wolf them all down the minute you get home from the store. They freeze well. When they get stale, they make great teething rings.

According to some sources, some enterprising baker first created the bagel in Central Europe in the early seventeenth century. A document from 1610 Poland mentions "beygls" given to women in the throes of labor. Maybe these "beygls" were indeed our heavenly rings of bread, or perhaps they were something entirely different. Regardless, it's plain that from the very start of the history of bagels, they were associated with Jewish mamas. I'd like to think that a Jewish mother's first reward for the trials of childbirth was a bagel warm from the oven.

Now, here's something that every Jewish mother has strong feelings about: a bagel's style. The two most prominent styles of traditional bagel in North America are the Montreal bagel and the New York bagel.

The Montreal bagel:
* Contains malt and egg but no salt
* Is boiled in honey-sweetened water before being baked in a wood oven
* Has poppy or sesame seeds
* Is smaller, chewier, and sweeter than the New York bagel
* Has a larger hole than the New York bagel

The New York bagel:
* Contains salt and malt
* Is boiled in honey-sweetened water before being baked in a wood oven
* May or may not have poppy or sesame seeds (as well as other embellishments and flavors)
* Is puffy with a noticeable crust and is less sweet than the Montreal bagel
* Has a smaller hole than the Montreal bagel

As all Jewish mothers realize, neither type of bagel is better or worse; this is a matter of taste. Not everything about bagels is as clear-cut, however.

Accept Only Authentic Bagels

As you've already read, Jewish mothers know that bagels are an appropriate snack morning, noon, and night. Bagels carry an important warning, however: There are bagels and then there are round breadlike things with holes in the middle. These rolls-with-a-hole are *not* bagels—especially if they come in a plastic bag and have been previously frozen. It's the same with movie stars: like bagels, they're often confused. For instance, people confuse Michael Jackson and Diana Ross. They're not the same. Likewise, people confuse Alan Cumming and Paul Reubens. They're not the same either, although the latter *is* Jewish. Likewise, a bagel is *not* a roll-with-a-hole.

The Bialy

A bialy is another yummy traditional Jewish bread product. Relatively flat, it is less crisp on the outside than a bagel. Most important of all, it doesn't have a hole and is often onion- or garlic-flavored, requiring a breath mint after consumption.

McDonald's created a line of bagel sandwiches for its breakfast menu. These are not bagels, even though they are called bagels. You think you can find bagels in your frozen food case. These are not bagels. A REAL bagel has a dense, chewy, doughy interior with a browned and sometimes crisp exterior. As any Jewish mother will tell you, accept no imitations.

A Bagel for Every Palate

Today, you can get bagels in just about any flavor you can imagine, from the classic onion, garlic, and salt to the new wave blueberry, strawberry, and multigrain. On St. Patrick's day, many shops produce green bagels. They're a bit odd, I have to admit, because they are so very green. And that's not all: Bagel toppings have become creative, too. Aside from the traditional sesame and poppy, bagels can be coated in just about anything you can imagine.

All of this is acceptable to the general Jewish bagel-loving populace, although old-line purists will decry any unconventional bagel, such as blueberry, as an abomination.

The Portable Jewish Mother

Glossary of Yiddish

"I don't speak Yiddish," you complain. I'll betcha you know a lot more Yiddish than you think. So stop your kvetching and read on.

Have you heard this one?

A Jewish mother walks her son to the school-bus corner on his first day of kindergarten. As she bends down to kiss him, she says; "Behave, my bubbulah. Take good care of yourself and think about the importance of your studies. Bubbulah, promise me to be a good boy in school and work hard. Listen to the teacher, bubbulah, and play nice with the other kids.

"My dearest bubbulah, remember not to run in the streets; God forbid you should get hit by a car. Also, bubbulah, don't forget to bring your snack. I made a nice tuna sandwich for you and put in a piece of fruit. And my darling bubbulah, don't forget that Mommy loves you very much."

At the end of the school day the bus comes back. The Jewish mother runs to her son and hugs him.

"So what did my bubbulah learn on his first day of school?" she asks.

The boy answers, "I learned my name is David."

The Portable Jewish Mother

You Already Know Some Yiddish

Yiddish is an unusual language because so few people really speak it yet many people—especially Jewish mothers—know a lot of Yiddish words. A case in point is the word bubbulah, which is an endearing term for anyone you like, young or old. Many Yiddish words have become part of English. I'll bet you know a lot more Yiddish than you realize.

So how much Yiddish do you know? Take this simple test to see. Circle the definition for each numbered and boldfaced Yiddish word.

Spelling

Because Yiddish is transcribed into English, spellings differ, depending on who's doing the transcribing. *Bubbulah*, for instance, is also *bubelah*, *bubalah*, and so on. Bear this in mind when you write Yiddish; it has some flexibility.

Spanish/English Bilingual Education—No Way!

There may be those among you who support making Spanish an official language in America. I for one am dead-set against it. We must preserve the sanctity of the English language. We cannot let foreign words creep into English.

To all the (1) **schlemiels and nudnicks** who are out there lurking in the crowd, I want to say that I for one get very sentimental when I think about English and its place at the heart of American society.

To tell you the truth, thinking about getting rid of English makes me so (2) **farklempt** that I'm fit to (3) **plotz**. When I hear these experts (4) **kvetching** about our national language, the whole (5) **schmeer** just gives me heartburn. Burp. What (6) **chutzpah** they have to try to change English!

These (7) **nebbishes** can tout their opinions about the cultural and linguistic diversity of our great country and of English itself, but I for one am not buying their (8) **shtick**. It's just (9) **dreck** as far as I'm concerned. I exhort you all to be (10) **menschen** about this and stand up for pure English, unadulterated by foreign words and expressions. It wouldn't be kosher to do anything else.

Remember, when it's all said and done, we have our great language of English and they've got (11) **bupkis**! At this point, the whole debate is a pain in the (12) **tuchus**!

258

Can You Talk the Talk?

1. schlemiels and nudnicks
   A. washed-up opera singers
   B. cross-dressers
   C. fools, nerds

2. farklempt
   A. delighted
   B. well-dressed
   C. upset

3. plotz
   A. applaud
   B. convert
   C. bust a gut

4. kvetching
   A. muttering
   B. gossiping
   C. complaining

5. schmeer
   A. rutabaga
   B. hamburger
   C. affair, thing

6. chutzpah
   A. weakness
   B. cowardice
   C. nerve, gall

7. nebbishes
   A. experts
   B. hunks of burning love
   C. more nerds

8. shtick
   A. lobster
   B. razor
   C. performance

9. dreck
   A. politics as usual
   B. gold
   C. garbage

10. menschen
    A. hoodlums
    B. foreigners
    C. respected people

11. bupkis
    A. burps
    B. carrots
    C. nothing

12. tuchus
    A. brain
    B. boobs
    C. butt

Every answer is C.
1–3 correct: Oy! You only know a bissel (a little) Yiddish.
4–6 correct: Get yourself a nosh (snack); you earned it.
7–10 correct: Such a maven! (expert)

The Importance of Yiddish
Do you know this one?

> On a bus in Tel Aviv, a Jewish mother was talking animatedly in Yiddish to her little boy, who kept answering her in Hebrew.
> And each time the mother said, "No, no, talk Yiddish!" An impatient Israeli, overhearing this, exclaimed, "Lady, why do you insist the boy talk Yiddish instead of Hebrew?"
> Replied the mother, "I don't want him to forget he's a Jew."

Why is Yiddish important to the Jewish people? Why is it so characteristic of Jewish mothers? After all, it's not the official language of Israel—Hebrew has that distinction. Yiddish isn't even widely spoken. Jews in France are more likely to speak French than Yiddish; Jews in Argentina are more likely to speak Spanish than

The Portable Jewish Mother

Yiddish. But Yiddish fulfills several important functions in Jewish culture.

Mamaloshen by Mandy Patinkin

If you want to hear some classic Jewish songs sung with more than a touch of schmaltz, get the CD of Mandy Patinkin's *Mamaloshen*. Patinkin also created Yiddish versions of "Supercalifragilisticexpialidocious," "Take Me Out to the Ballgame," and "The Hokey Pokey," showing that Yiddish has wide appeal.

Yiddish Creates Cultural Unity

First, Yiddish is a force that binds Jews together, in a much better way than matzoh binds our bowels during Passover. Yiddish is the *mamaloshen*—the mother tongue, the traditional language of the Jewish home and hearth. As Jewish mothers unify our families, so Yiddish helps unify our culture. Even Jews who don't "speak" Yiddish know at least a handful of Yiddish words from their families. My introduction to Yiddish came from my father, who liked to sing this off-color ditty: "Schmeckle, schmeckle, don't you cry. You'll be a big putz by and by."

Cleaned up, it means: "Silly fool, don't cry; you'll be total jerk soon."

Yiddish Is Precise

My friend Betty Gold always says that if you can't provide the word for something, you can't describe it. She argues that you must assign the precise word to an object to know the object. She's right. Yiddish is a language that allows accuracy. It gives us the words to provide the exact shades of meaning we require. Jewish mothers recognize the need for accuracy, especially when berating their children.

You may have heard that Eskimos have hundreds of words for "snow." They don't, but Yiddish has many words for "fools." The following chart illustrates my point. Check out the different connotations and shades of meaning that each word carries.

Insult Your Friends with Precision

Yiddish Term for Fool	Meaning	Insult Scale (1–10)
klutz	clumsy person	1
nudnick	pest	2
nebbish	nerd	2
luftmensch	dreamer	3
schlemiel	hopeless bungler	4
pisher	a nobody	4

The Portable Jewish Mother

schnook	sad sack	4
schlemozel	unlucky person	5
schmendrick	idiot	5
schlub	a clumsy, stupid, or unattractive person	6
shmegege	stupid person	6
schmo	a stupid person (an alteration of schmuck)	7
schmuck	dope, jerk (a penis). I grew up thinking the word *shmuck* meant "lousy driver."	10
putz	jerk, ass (penis)	10
momzer	bastard (Often used affection-ately by grandfathers to address their grandchildren. Mine did. Don't ask me why.)	10

● ●

Such a Fool!

Having trouble keeping these words straight? According to the old joke, the shmegege is the one who cleans up the soup the schlemiel spilled on the schlemozel.

● ●

Yiddish Is Colorful

And when it comes to cursing, you can't beat Yiddish. The next time someone cuts you off on the road, fella, pull your pants up to your nipples, head for the 4:30 dinner special, and bellow out some of these:

* May all your teeth fall out except one, so that you can have a toothache, God forbid.
* May your liver come out of your nostrils piece by piece.
* May you be like a lamp: hang by day, burn by night, and be snuffed out in the morning.
* May you every day eat chopped liver with onions, herring, chicken soup with matzoh balls, carp with horseradish, roast beef with tsimmes (a sweet side dish), pancakes, and tea with lemon—and may you choke on every bite.
* May the only thing anyone ever writes you be a prescription.
* May you have the juiciest goose, but no teeth; the best wine, but no sense of taste; the most beautiful wife, but no virility.

The History of Yiddish

Yiddish arose about a thousand years ago from Middle High German, spreading throughout the ghettos of central and eastern

Europe, borrowing words from the countries in which the Jews lived. Thus, it incorporates words from Hebrew, Russian, Polish and other Slavic languages, Romance languages, and later, English. About 70–75 percent of the words in Yiddish come from German.

Before World War II, Yiddish was spoken by 11 million to 13 million people. Today, it is spoken by perhaps one-tenth as many. But that's okay, because so many Yiddish words and phrases have become a part of English, as you've learned. Likely that's because Yiddish says it so well.

The Roots of Yiddish

The oldest surviving literary document in Yiddish is a blessing in a Hebrew prayer book from 1272:

Transliterated: Gut tak im betage se vaer dis makhazor in beis hakneses terage.

Translated: May a good day come to him who carries this prayer book into the synagogue.

This saying shows that Yiddish was similar to Middle High German, into which Hebrew words had been included.

We can date some of the earliest songs and poems in Yiddish to the 1300s and 1400s. The printing press helped spread Yiddish across Europe. Since Jewish mothers usually didn't read Hebrew but did read and write Yiddish, nonreligious Yiddish literature developed for women.

The Golden Age of Yiddish Literature

The late 1800s and early 1900s saw the golden age of secular Yiddish literature. The three most important writers were:

* Sholem Yankev Abramovitch, writing as Mendele Mocher Sforim
* Sholem Yakov Rabinovitsh, known as Shalom Aleichem, author of *Tevye the Milkman*, the basis for *Fiddler on the Roof*
* Isaac Leib Peretz

* *

Shalom Aleichem

The pen name Shalom Aleichem comes from the common greeting meaning "peace be with you."

* *

Yiddish in the Twentieth Century

Around 1900, Yiddish became widely spoken in Eastern Europe. Yiddish even became one of the official languages of the Belorussian USSR—and the Soviets were not known for their friendliness toward the Jews. Yiddish flourished on the stage, in literature, and in films. Cause and effect are slippery here: Did Yiddish become more popular because of Yiddish theater and film or did its popularity result in more theater and film? Regardless, Yiddish language classes were offered in schools, so Yiddish became even more widely spoken and read. Another result of these classes was a movement toward uniform and codified Yiddish spelling.

As you would expect, the Holocaust saw a tragic and sudden reduction in the number of Yiddish speakers. That's because Yiddish had been spoken in many of the communities the Nazis destroyed. A significant number of the survivors did not seek to speak Yiddish, preferring to blend into their adoptive countries.

Today, Yiddish is once again popular, especially among Israelis, even though they may not be religious. In Israel, Yiddish theater has a devoted following, with the dialogue presented on stage in Yiddish and translated into Hebrew and Russian. Universities offer Yiddish classes, too.

In America, people continue to speak, write, and publish in Yiddish, most notably the Hasidic Jews. Many Hasidic Jews live in Brooklyn's Borough Park, Williamsburg, and Crown Heights.

In addition, there are more than 100 Yiddish newspapers, magazines, and radio programs around the worldwide. As you would expect, Yiddish has a cyberspace presence as well, shown by the numerous Yiddish Web sites, listservs, and blogs.

Chai

In Judaism, the chai symbol consists of the two Hebrew letters chet and yod. The word means "life." Chet has the numeric value of 8; yod is worth 10, for a total of 18. Thus, it is considered good luck to give gifts of money in multiples of 18. Did you notice how many chapters there are in this book?

Leo Rosten

Any discussion of Yiddish must start by paying homage to the masterful writer and humorist Leo Rosten (1908–1997). Here are some of Rosten's most notable accomplishments:

* *The Education of H*Y*M*A*N K*A*P*L*A*N*, tales of night-school "prodigy" Hyman Kaplan.
* *The Joys of Yiddish,* still the number-one best volume that I've ever found on the subject. (And don't e-mail me that you've found a better one. I will always be an unabashed Leo Rosten groupie.)
* *Hooray for Yiddish!*, a funny lexicon of the American language as influenced by Jewish culture.
* *Leo Rosten's Treasury of Jewish Quotations.*

The Portable Jewish Mother

Yinglish

The term "Yinglish" was coined to describe the distinctive way that certain Jews in English-speaking countries add many Yiddish words into their conversation, beyond general Yiddish words commonly used. Many of these words have not been assimilated into English and are unlikely to be understood by English speakers who don't have a substantial Yiddish background.

Yiddish Inflection

Inflection is a vital part of using Yiddish authentically, like a lantsman (a member of the tribe). I adapted information from Leo Rosten's wonderful book *The Joys of Yiddish* for the following guide to speaking Yiddish with the proper body language.

You'll notice that there's no Yiddish at all in the following examples. This is deliberate: I want to ease you into the language slowly.

As you read each sentence, put the emphasis on the word in boldface. As you repeat these phrases, work some shoulder shrugging, frowning, and eyebrow raising into the action. The first column has the sentence; the second column, the meaning. As you'll notice, the meaning of the same sentence changes completely depending on the word you emphasize.

The Emphasis Is All

Sentence	Meaning
I should buy two tickets for her dance recital?	After the shabby way she acted toward me I should spend my money on her?
I *should* buy two tickets for her dance recital?	So now you're giving me a lesson in moral values?
I should *buy* two tickets for her dance recital?	I wouldn't go even if she were giving out free tickets.
I should buy *two* tickets for her dance recital?	I'm having enough trouble deciding whether it's worth one.
I should buy two *tickets* for her dance recital?	She better hand out free tickets or the auditorium will be empty.
I should buy two tickets for *her* dance recital?	Did she buy tickets to our daughter's recital? I think not.
I should buy two tickets for her *dance recital?*	What? They call what she does "dance"?

Fortune

Jewish mothers have been quoting this Yiddish saying for centuries: "If fortune calls, give him a seat."

The Portable Jewish Mother

Learning Yiddish

A rabbi was opening his mail one morning. Taking a single sheet of paper from an envelope, he found only one word written on it: *schmuck*. At the next Friday night service, the rabbi announced, "I have known many people who have written letters and forgot to sign their names, but this week I received a letter from someone who signed his name . . . . and forgot to write a letter."

As your Jewish mother would command, learn some basic Yiddish words because:

* It's good for you.
* I told you so.
* Then you can understand what your father and I are talking about behind your back.

Dickhead

In 1998, Charles Schumer and Al D'Amato were running for the position of senior U.S. senator representing New York. During the race, D'Amato referred to Schumer as a putzhead. The *New York Times* referenced the entry for "putz" in *The Joys of Yiddish* and maintained that the phrase did not merely mean "fool," as D'Amato insisted, but was significantly more pejorative. Based on Rosten's entry in *The Joys of Yiddish*, a better translation might be "dickhead."

D'Amato ended up losing the race, and some observers credit this incident with costing him the election.

Time to master some Yiddish words for behavior. That way, you can join the legions of Jewish mothers who describe their children so precisely, lavishly, and constantly.

Fifteen Yiddish Words for Behavior

Word	Pronunciation	Meaning
alter kocker	OLL-ter KOCK-er	old fart; an old, cranky man
chazzer	KHAHZ-zer	pig, greedy person
chutzpah	KHOOTZ-pah	ballsiness, guts, daring, audacity
farblondzhet	fer-BLUNJ-it	lost, bewildered, confused
faygeleh	FAY-geh-leh	homosexual; effeminate
hock	HOCK	bother, pester
kibitz	KIB-itz	to offer unwanted advice
klutz	KLOTZ	clumsy person
kvetch	KVETCH	to complain habitually, gripe
macher	MOKH-er	big wheel
maven	MAY-vin	expert
mensch	MENCH	an upright man; a decent human

The Portable Jewish Mother

meshugge	m-SHU-geh	crazy
schnorrer	SHNOR-rer	beggar or person always asking others for a handout
shikkered	SHICK-erd	drunk, intoxicated

I Sing the Body Electric

Groucho Marx, the famous actor, wanted to join a beach club. His friend told him he'd never be approved for membership because the club didn't allow Jews. Groucho said, "My wife isn't Jewish, so will they let our son go into the water up to his knees?"

Below are some Yiddish words for body parts. As a good Jewish mother, you'll want to point out the bits that need washing.

Five Yiddish Words for Body Parts

Word	Pronunciation	Meaning
kishkes	KISH-keh	intestines; often applied to a woman's internal plumbing
punim	POON-im	face
pupik	PU-pik	navel
schlong	SHLONG	penis
tuchus	TOOK-is	buttocks

Oy Vey Ist Mir!

A Jewish mother can't manage without her Oy! It's an all-purpose Yiddish word that expresses joy, sadness, contentment, fear, astonishment, horror—and everything in between. If you want to get fancy, try "oy gevalt!" (Oh no!) and "oy vay!" (Oh, woe!) "Oy vey ist mir!" is varsity level; it means "Oh, woe am I!"

Below is a list of handy words and expressions that you can sprinkle into your conversation. They'll help you talk the talk as you walk the walk.

Fifteen Useful Yiddish Words and Expressions

Word	Pronunciation	Meaning
chozzerai	khoz-zair-EYE	junk, garbage, junk food
chutzpah	KHOOTS-pah	gall, brazen nerve
goy	GOY	someone not of the Jewish faith or people
kine-ahora	kane-a-HAW-reh	a phrase spoken to ward off the evil eye
mazel tov!	MOZ-el TOF	Congratulations! Good Luck! (*Mazel* means luck.) It's often said to avert a curse after something or someone has been praised.

The Portable Jewish Mother

nu	NOO	multipurpose interjection along the lines of "Well?" or "So?"
schlock	SHLOCK	shoddy, cheaply made article
shaygetz	SHAY-gets	gentile male
shiksa	SHK-seh	gentile woman
shul	SHOOL	synagogue
tchotchke	TSAHT-keh	knickknack, trinket
tsuris	TSOO-riss	troubles, suffering
yenta	YEN-ta	a talkative woman; a gossip; a blabbermouth; a scold
yontif	YUN-tiff	holiday
zaftig	ZOFF-tig	juicy, plump, full-figured woman

Test Yourself

I know you've got it, bubbulah, but practice makes perfect. Take this simple quiz to test your knowledge of Yiddish.

Directions: Circle the letter of the correct choice.

You're Sounding Like a
Member of the Tribe

1 Which of the following Jewish mothers is best described as zaftig?

A. Lisa Kudrow ("Phoebe") from *Friends*

B. Tori Spelling from *Beverly Hills 90210*

C. Julia Louis-Dreyfus ("Elaine") from *Seinfeld*

D. Roseanne Barr

2 Which of these won't you find on your body, assuming that the 85-year-old man next to you at the salad bar isn't copping a feel?

A. punim

B. pupik

C. tuchus

D. alter kocker

3 Your blind date, a brain surgeon, arrives with a box of pastry for your mother, holds open the door of his Mercedes